Sustainable Landscape P......

This book takes as its starting point the need to examine critically the case for landscape reconnection. It looks at alleged disconnections and their supposed consequences. It explores the arguments about reconnecting the natural and human elements of whole landscapes. More broadly, it considers landscape as an arena within which science, humanities and professions can find common ground, and in which vivid social learning can occur about key social and environmental issues. It takes a dynamic view of landscape, in contrast to the popular image of timeless, traditional scenery. It accepts that even the most cherished cultural landscapes will change and, indeed, it views 'change drivers' as a potentially positive means of creating new connectivities between people and place. It recognises the growing interest in promoting resilience and ecosystem services across extensive landscapes – such as by creating new 'space' for water and wildlife.

Paul Selman is Emeritus Professor of Landscape at the University of Sheffield, where he was formerly Head of Department. He has published extensively on landscape, environmental management and sustainable development, and has undertaken research for a range of government agencies as well as Research Councils.

Sustainable Landscape Planning

The Reconnection Agenda

Paul Selman

Routledge
Taylor & Francis Group

LONDON AND NEW YORK

First published 2012
by Routledge
2 Park Square, Milton Park, Abingdon, Oxon, OX14 4RN

Simultaneously published in the USA and Canada
by Routledge
711 Third Avenue, New York, NY 10017

Routledge is an imprint of the Taylor & Francis Group, an informa business

British Library Cataloguing in Publication Data
A catalogue record for this book is available from the British Library

Library of Congress Cataloging-in-Publication Data
Selman, Paul H.
Sustainable landscape planning : the reconnection agenda / Paul Selman.
    p. cm.
  "Simultaneously published in the USA and Canada"–T.p. verso.
  Includes bibliographical references and index.
  1. Ecological landscape design. 2. Ecological landscape design–
  Europe. 3. Sustainable development–Planning. 4. Sustainable
  development–Europe–Planning. 5. Landscape ecology. 6. Landscape
  ecology–Europe. 7. Landscape protection. 8. Landscape protection–
  Europe. 9. Land use–Environmental aspects. 10. Land use–
  Environmental aspects–Europe. I. Title.
SB472.45.S45 2012
658.4′083–dc23   2012000773

ISBN: 978-1-84971-262-0 (hbk)
ISBN: 978-1-84971-263-7 (pbk)
ISBN: 978-0-203-11986-0 (ebk)

Typeset in Sabon
by HWA Text and Data Management, London

Printed and bound in Great Britain by
TJ International Ltd, Padstow, Cornwall

Contents

Figures

Tables

Boxes

Chapter 1

Landscape – connections and disconnections

Introduction

Most people feel they have a reasonably clear idea of what landscape means. Typically, they think of fine scenery, a painting, a designed garden, an urban park, or perhaps their local green spaces. In reality, even people who claim to be specialists in landscape rarely understand its full range of meanings. Landscape architects, landscape ecologists, cultural geographers, physical geographers, art historians, spatial planners, archaeologists, social psychologists and others use the term in very different ways and often have blind spots about each other's theories and methods. Landscape is a term that is both disputed between specialists and also difficult to translate between languages.

The origins of the term 'landscape' have been widely discussed. Writers agree that the most influential terms have been the German 'landschäft' and the Dutch 'landschap' (or, archaically, 'landskab'). It has been suggested that these are, respectively, a geographically 'bounded area' and a more visual or artistic 'perceived area'. Wylie (2007) helpfully explores the ambiguities in these apparently simple distinctions. Different nuances of these terms, and their equivalents in various languages, may imply additional ideas about ownership and belonging, regional identity, and physical morphology. As Wylie notes, dictionary definitions typically converge on the idea of landscape being a portion of land or scenery that the eye can view at once. This notion conflicts, however, with scholarly and professional practices that study landscape ecological processes over ranges of many kilometres, map landscape character across regions, or deconstruct unseen qualities that contribute to 'place'.

Broadly speaking, different conceptions of landscape locate themselves along a spectrum from a visual and painterly view at one end, where a framed scene with selectively foregrounded features is captured for an admiring gaze, to a more inhabited concept of landscape at the other, where people, land and history combine to create a sense of belonging associated with a mappable region. The extremes overlap extensively – a landscape painting is often of greatest interest for the people, customs or work that it depicts, whilst landscapes noted for their distinctive culture and history will often also be recognizable by their scenery.

Many languages lack a term that adequately translates landscape. Problems even arise in Europe between the Germanic north's landschäft (landscape, landschap, etc.) and the Romance south's paysage (paesaggio, paisaje, etc.), whose meanings differ significantly. Over the past century or so, the scientific appropriation of landscape has added new complexities. Geomorphologists refer to landscape as the physical nature of the earth's surface, on which formative processes operate. Ecologists see landscape as a land–water area larger than the habitat, across which species act out their life-cycle processes of birth, immigration, death and emigration; whilst archaeologists conceive of an area beyond the individual site or monument that is infused with a complementary time-depth. Sustainability scientists refer to landscape as a space possessing multifunctional properties that integrate natural and human ecosystem services, whilst resilience scientists view landscape as an encompassing social–ecological system that is vulnerable to destabilization. Behavioural scientists understand landscape as a human life-space that provides us with affordances for survival and pleasure, and which affect our behaviour, mood and well-being. In terms of creative enterprise, throughout most of civilization, skilled designers have converted land into landscape, using physical materials and plants to create gardens, parks, demesnes, squares and other private and public spaces.

This book concerns the cultural landscape, a term that also lends itself to endless dispute. The European Landscape Convention (Council of Europe, 2000) has defined landscape as an area, as perceived by people, whose character is the result of the action and interaction of natural and/or human factors – a definition that is now widely accepted by practitioners, although scholars would dissect it mercilessly. Pragmatically, however, it is a useful working definition. The overriding feature is that 'culture' combines with 'nature', so that human agency becomes an important driver of a landscape's appearance and functionality (Figure 1.1).

Landscape is different from scenery, although in popular language they are rarely separated; even in policy and technical language the two may be conflated. Scenery is essentially visual – it may simply be enjoyed as a sweep of countryside, or it may be mapped by techniques that identify its characteristics and possibly even quantify its relative importance. The visual qualities of landscape – delightful or dramatic scenery, generally combined with 'picture postcard' villages – have, in practice, dominated spatial planning and environmental management policy, despite the occasional statement suggesting a more sophisticated view. Yi-Fu Tuan (1977) has also shown how 'scenery' is in part imaginary and illusory, comparable to a staged performance in drama. More recent researchers have emphasized how landscapes have been appropriated and airbrushed, so that they can be commodified for commercial purposes such as promoting tourism and speciality foods.

Figure 1.1   The Peak District National Park, UK: a classic example of a relatively wild landscape that has evolved through an interplay between physical geography and human activities

Landscape, even as a painterly artifice or as a designed area of public realm, comprises far more than the visual, although, given the primacy of sight amongst the senses, it is usually something that people intuitively 'perceive'. In addition to its perceived properties, however, landscape is rich with stories, nutrient cycles, carbon fluxes, customary laws, economic activities and manifold other mysteries. The crises faced by many landscapes, and the potential of landscape to frame lives, livelihoods, scientific enquiry and public policy, cannot be understood within a narrowly visual conception. An understanding of landscape must go 'beyond the view' (Countryside Agency, 2006). The multifaceted nature of landscape – comprising a spectrum of interconnected relationships, practices and processes – is summarised in Table 1.1 and Figure 1.2.

The disconnected landscape

This book addresses a core challenge facing contemporary cultural landscapes. The landscape is more than mere scenery – it is a complex system comprising natural and social subsystems. Its properties derive from

Table 1.1 Cultural landscape: the seen and unseen (based on Countryside Agency, 2006; Stephenson, 2007)

	Practices	Processes	Relationships
Experience	• the experience of health and well-being • creating places that have meaning and identity • hefting and traversing	• localization of culture • globalization of culture • place-making	• meanings, memories, stories and symbolism • aesthetic and spiritual qualities • sense of belonging • in-dwelling
History	• remanence of former activities and structures	• decay and renewal	• genealogical links • laws and customs
Land use	• construction • farming, forestry and other land management • energy production and transmission • communication networks	• human influences on air, water and soil dynamics	• formal land ownership and rights • cultural expectations regarding wise use and access across all land
Natural form	• land drainage and regrading • restoration and reclamation	• landform evolution • soil development and degradation • coastal processes	• sacred sites • inspirational qualities of hills, coastline etc.
Wildlife	• wildlife management • effects of other land uses on biodiversity • reintroduction and re-wilding	• life-cycle processes of wild species	• ethical attitudes towards nature • cultural perceptions of 'weed' and 'pest' species

the dynamic relations between these subsystems, producing a whole that is more than the sum of the parts. Both in terms of their visual coherence and their unseen processes, landscapes have generally become more 'disconnected' in ways that compromise their character, sustainability and resilience. A unifying goal of policy, planning and science is thus to reconnect landscapes in a range of physical and social ways. Physical reconnections, for example, entail joining up vegetated networks within an ecological habitat matrix; social ones may involve recovering links between people and place.

There is a widely held acknowledgement that cultural landscapes have become fragmented, homogenised and impoverished (Jongman, 2002). Building on this view, it has often been suggested that the disruption of

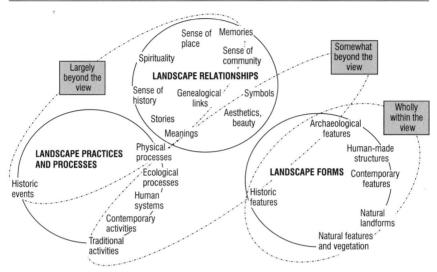

Figure 1.2 Cultural landscape: seen and unseen forms, relationships, practices and processes (based on Countryside Agency, 2006; Stephenson, 2007)

systems that make up the physical landscape, and the erosion of bonds between people and place, might lie at the source of much environmental and social malaise. Unfortunately, these claims have often been made in an assertive way, supported by essentialist arguments about the need for people to 'reconnect' with the earth and with the 'spirit of the place'. This book seeks to offer a more evidence-based case for such arguments; it draws upon a wide range of disciplines regarding the alleged disconnection of landscape, and the theoretical and practical basis for reconnection.

Some of the key types of 'disconnect' that have been claimed include:

- loss of attachment between people and the place in which they dwell;
- loss of connection between people and nature;
- loss of connections between past and present, eroding the memories and meanings of landscape;
- loss of connectivity between ecological habitats;
- loss of linkages within and between ground and surface waters;
- dis-embedding of economic activity from its platial setting;
- lack of effective connectivity in low carbon transport networks;
- loss of connection between town and country.

Variously, these have been associated with declining landscape character, over-exploitation of land and nature, urban flooding, diminishing biodiversity, antisocial behaviour, reduced sense of personal agency, unsustainable modes of energy use and transport, and deteriorating health, fitness and well-being. Indeed, many of the environmental problems around the world have been attributed to a profound disconnection between humankind and nature: it is argued that our reductionist tradition has led us to gaze exploitatively on the environment as neutral and profitable stuff, rather than to see ourselves as an inextricable and non-dominant part of 'nature'.

Hence, various types of reconnection have been advocated, to create sense of place, sustainable drainage, ecological networks, embedded economies, healthier lives and adaptive communities. One of the key problems in justifying such measures, however, is that the evidence for loss of connection and the potential for reconnection is often weak and unconvincing. The idea of local communities identifying with a distinctive landscape is perhaps no more than a yearned-for myth. Indeed, some critics oppose the pursuit of localism, not least because 'communities of place' can be bastions of parish-pump narrow-mindedness.

This book takes as its starting point the need to examine critically the case for landscape reconnection. It looks at alleged disconnections and their supposed consequences. It explores the arguments about reconnecting the natural and human elements of whole landscapes. More broadly, it considers landscape as an arena within which science, humanities and professions can find common ground, and in which vivid social learning can occur about key social and environmental issues. It takes a dynamic view of landscape, in contrast to the popular image of timeless, traditional scenery. It accepts that even the most cherished cultural landscapes will change and, indeed, it views 'change drivers' as a potentially positive means of creating new connectivities between people and place. It recognizes the growing interest in creating new 'space' for wildlife and water, since reconnection cannot occur unless there is sufficient elbow room for system processes to establish a dynamic equilibrium. In many countries, government policies are now starting to recognize a need for connection and multifunctionality – an important expression of this in the UK is summarized in Box 1.1.

The terms 'nature', 'culture', 'social' and 'ecological' are used extensively throughout this book. These are all highly contested terms about which much has been written in the context of various disciplines. Here, they are often used as shorthand for more complex ideas, and are to be treated as convenient metaphors rather than as definitive concepts. In this book, 'nature' is used simply to refer to everything in the landscape that is non-human. It does not necessarily draw upon the body of scholarship about the social construction of 'nature' and the commodification of non-human species. 'Culture' is used broadly to refer to things that people do and think, as well as the material traces and intangible imprints that they leave on the landscape. 'Social' may, particularly in the context of social–ecological systems, include all human processes, such as social organization, economic production and trade, the built environment, health and behaviour. 'Ecological' similarly includes more than biodiversity, and in places is taken to include all the physical environmental systems that support life.

Box 1.1   Guidance to UK politicians on multifunctional landscape (Parliamentary Office of Science and Technology, 2011)

Advice to UK politicians points out that traditional approaches to land use have focused on single, mono-functional purposes, often with negative consequences. For example:

- many food production systems will not be viable in the long term due to heavy reliance on fertilizers and fossil fuels, soil degradation and emissions of greenhouse gases, and thus need to be redesigned;
- wildlife sites contribute in very important ways to ecosystem services but they are highly fragmented, mostly too small, insufficiently protected and under-managed;
- green belts are designated to prevent urban sprawl but can promote 'leapfrogging' of development, leading to longer commuting and bigger urban footprints.

The advice note suggests the promotion of multifunctional landscapes, wherein a single area of land can deliver multiple ecosystem services, and it identifies national planning policy guidance as a basis for coordinating land uses and securing continuity across administrative boundaries.

The following sections introduce some key concepts relating to human and physical connections in the landscape. These provide a basic terminology and conceptual repertoire for later chapters.

Human connections and the landscape: some preliminary terminology

Biophilia, restoration and aesthetics

Clearly, humans need 'nature' to provide basic requirements such as food and water. However, it is likely that we also have less visible needs. Wilson (1984) proposed a hypothesis known as 'biophilia', which looked beyond the basic role of nature in satisfying our physical wants. This hypothesis was used to suggest that humans have an innate, hereditary attachment to nature that means we need it not only for essential physical requirements, but also for aesthetic, intellectual, cognitive and spiritual meaning and satisfaction. If this is true, then we have a natural instinct, which is evolutionary and inherited, to desire contact with nature. Further, it seems to be important in guaranteeing genetic fitness and competitive advantage, as well as contributing to personal identity and fulfilment (Newton, 2007). Pigram

(1993) has suggested that humans have a genetically coded predisposition to respond positively to content in the natural environment.

Evolutionary biology suggests that detachment from something that was necessary to our survival and comfort, but which has now become unavailable, might cause a discord between preferred and actual environment (Grinde, 2009). Thus, our environment of evolutionary adaptedness (EEA) has had an important impact on the evolution of the human brain (Grinde and Grindal Patil, 2009). Sometimes, the way we actually live our lives is in conflict with the way of life for which we are genetically designed – these deviations have been referred to as mismatches. Some of these are beneficial, such as sleeping on a mattress instead of on the ground, but others may be detrimental, and may contribute to disease or reduce our quality of life. The latter are referred to as discords, and they have a negative impact that, in susceptible individuals, will cause some form of stress (Grinde and Grindal Patil, 2009). Discords may impair well-being, and some psychologists have suggested that they may be remedied by an increased 'dose' of the missing qualities. Although any organ or bodily function can suffer from discords, the human brain appears to be particularly vulnerable due to its complexity, and its need to mature over a long period in response to environmental stimuli. It seems likely that vegetation is agreeable, and that the absence of greenery is sensed, possibly unconsciously, as a stress factor. This has been suggested as an important contributor to the high incidence of mental disorders in Western societies. Kellert (1993) has proposed a useful classification of the different biological bases on which we might relate to the natural environment (Box 1.2).

Most studies dealing with the psychological benefits of nature lie within the field of environmental psychology, and are typically based on ideas about the effects of contact with naturalistic environments. The most widely studied effect is that of 'restoration', which refers to the process of regaining psychological, social and physical capacity. Kaplan and Kaplan's (1989) attention restoration theory and Ulrich's (1983) psychophysiological stress reduction framework offer similar ways of explaining restorative psychological benefits. Throughout our daily lives, we direct our attention to demanding tasks and deal with disturbing environmental factors, resulting in mental fatigue. By contrast, environments that provide a possibility for more effortless attention may help to restore our mental capacity. Surroundings dominated by elements of nature are thought to be restorative, and some psychologists argue that physical or visual contact with nature can promote high-order cognitive functioning, thereby enhancing our observational skills and ability to reason.

A very influential explanation of the concept of a 'restorative environment' – where the recovery of mental energies and effectiveness is enhanced – has been proposed by Kaplan and Kaplan (1989). In this, the natural environment is considered to have a special relationship to each of four factors that are important to a restorative experience. These are:

Box 1.2 The various ways in which humans might respond to nature (summarized from Kellert, 1993)

- utilitarian – the practical and material exploitation of nature for various human needs such as food;
- naturalistic – the satisfaction derived from direct contact with nature related to mental and physical development, for example our acquisition of outdoor skills;
- scientific – the systematic study of nature, to develop our knowledge and observational skills;
- aesthetic – the physical appeal of nature and its effect on our inspiration, calm and security;
- symbolic – the use of nature in language, metaphor and communication;
- humanistic – strong affection for and emotional attachment to nature;
- moralistic – reverence or ethical concern for nature, sometimes related to conduct and order;
- dominionistic – physical control and dominance of nature, developing our ability to regulate and 'tame' our surroundings;
- negativistic – fear of nature, and our ability to defend ourselves against it.

- being away – for an environment to be restorative one must feel a sense of distance and a feeling of escape from some aspects of life that are ordinarily present, notably, distractions, obligations, pursuits, purposes and thoughts;
- extent – the scope and connectedness of an environment that is extensive in time and space, and that is also sufficiently connected to allow us to construct an image of a larger whole;
- fascination – derived from the distinction between directed (voluntary) attention and involuntary attention, such that nature is assumed to act on the involuntary attention whilst the directed attention (which can be depleted) recovers; and
- compatibility – the fit between environment, the individual's inclination and their activities within the environment.

More subtly, the effect of nature on our level of attentiveness or fatigue may relate to subconscious cues. Thus, objects within the field of vision may exert an influence even if the conscious brain does not recognize their existence. Whilst the visual presence of plants may have a positive effect on well-being and health, perhaps also the absence of plants may suggest an unnatural, and thus potentially unsafe, environment. Non-visual aspects of plants, such as fragrance and improved acoustics, may also play a role (Gidlöf-Gunnarsson and Öhrström, 2007).

Miller (2005), writing about the 'extinction of experience' (Pyle, 1978) considered that most people's sensory experience has been seriously impoverished. He suggested that this was strongly related to the fact that around half of the world's people live in urban areas where they are increasingly disconnected from nature. For various reasons, he argued that the places where people live and work should be designed in ways that provide opportunities for meaningful interactions with the natural world. As well as enhancing our well-being, this could lead us to demand greener environments and attach higher priority to landscape creation and protection more generally. Miller noted that our development of land has had a homogenizing effect on biodiversity, greatly reducing native habitats and producing habitats that are dominated by a relatively small number of species suited to highly urbanized areas. In addition, whilst some native species do manage to remain in cities, they tend to be in sites away from the neighbourhoods where most people live. Hence, most people suffer biological impoverishment because they encounter biological uniformity in their day-to-day lives. This is compounded by a 'shifting baseline of environmental generational amnesia', because the environment encountered during our childhood becomes the baseline against which we evaluate our environment later in life, so that we continually ratchet down our expectations regarding the quality of natural areas closest to our homes and workplaces. Further, our pace of life is accelerating so that the rhythms of human activity, both in the overscheduled lives of adults and the 'virtual' play environments of children, become more and more different from those of the natural world. Thus, our 'extinction of experience' is characterized by a cycle of impoverishment initiated by the homogenization and reduction of local flora and fauna, and followed by emotional separation, disaffection and apathy. In turn, because we do not care for or demand ecologically rich neighbourhoods, we end up living in more biologically depauperate environments with still deeper isolation from nature.

Urban environments offer major opportunities for reconnection. Even though they may not contain many rare or exciting species, they do provide plenty of illustrations of ecological processes and, given suitable attention to aesthetic and conservation values, have the potential to engage a broad segment of the public. It also seems likely that people who establish personal connections with natural areas are more highly motivated to protect such environments. Thus, 'reconciliation ecologists' (Rosenzweig, 2003) have argued that partnerships between designers and ecologists, and those who actually live and work in places, can help to find ways of modifying urbanized habitats so that they meet human needs and also provide for nature. Kahn (1999) suggests that estrangement or disconnection from nature goes back to childhood, and so proposes involving children more actively in designing urban green space, and enabling them to forge their own connections with the natural world. It has been suggested that this will occur spontaneously if appropriate places are provided. Formal parks and traditional playgrounds are often inadequate for this purpose, whereas areas of undeveloped and unmanaged land close to the home might better enable children to realize their potential for self-teaching. Evidence indicates that children who play in wild environments show a greater affinity and appreciation for such places later in life.

Bauer et al. (2009) have looked at the contemporary experience of biophilia. In this regard, van den Born et al. (2001) referred to a 'new biophilia' whereby people typically feel that nature has a value of its own, and relatively few consider humans to be superior to nature. Specifically, Bauer et al. examined people's attitudes to the process of re-wilding, or the reversion of agriculturally improved land to semi-natural habitat. In places, this is occurring as a conscious policy choice, but in the upland areas of Switzerland, where the study took place, it is mainly an unplanned process resulting from the abandonment of hill farming. Its consequences for landscape can be summarized as:

- reduction or extinction of many species of flora and fauna linked with disappearing cultural diversity;
- change from fine towards coarse grained patterns of landscape;
- reduction or disappearance of open spaces and their transformation into dense scrub that in turn has negative consequences for the aesthetic value of cultural landscapes;
- merging of forested patches, resulting in an increased risk of wildfires;
- modification of geomorphological processes on slopes that increases the risk of soil erosion.

Bauer et al.'s findings identified four different expressions of biophilia amongst their survey group, namely, nature-connected users, nature sympathizers, nature controllers and nature lovers. The nature-connected users had a utilitarian attitude towards nature, yet considered themselves to be part of nature and felt emotionally close to it. They wished nature to be protected, and had a preference for gardens to look neat and manicured. The nature sympathizers were rather emotionally distanced from nature but did tend to be quite biophilic: they felt that diversity of nature was important, that nature does not have to please humans, and that controlling nature was not always the best way to prevent natural hazards. Nature controllers held more preservationist views about the protection of nature: they did not feel especially close to nature, and wanted to influence it so that it looked well kept and organized. The nature lovers attached very high priority to the diversity of nature and its pristine character, they felt a part of nature, and they supported the idea of leaving nature to develop more spontaneously and reducing human influence. The types differed significantly in terms of age, provenance (urban or rural), place of residence (urban or rural)

Table 1.2 Demographic factors that appear to influence our relationship to landscape (based on Natural England, 2009a)

Age	Slight variation in response to landscape depending on age and amassed experience – younger tend to be more interested in active recreational side of landscape experience, whilst older (or with stressful jobs) are more interested in aesthetic/calming/tranquillity benefits and associated landscape memories
Physical capabilities	Determined by age, health or disability – influences degree of dependence on facilities and access services, but does not necessarily stop enjoyment of the experience of the landscape or the desire to seek different landscape characteristics
Gender	Women more influenced than men by safety and security that may affect the places, times and circumstances in which visits (especially alone or with young children) are undertaken; slight differences in qualities sought; women more likely to be in company of children and so sense potential of landscape for play, stimulus, etc.
Situational	Availability of time and current life circumstances
Group composition or social context	Landscape experience is affected by social context – whether experienced with family members, friends, colleagues, strangers (such as when children make spontaneous friends when playing) or mainly on their own; influences mood, topics of discussion, etc.
Perspectives within the landscape	Some landscapes were preferred close-up (e.g. deciduous woodland), others from a distance (e.g. conifer plantations)
Awareness factors	Awareness of geology, history, wildlife habitats, etc. – increased familiarity with a place assisted 'sense of place' and reminiscing
Structure and function preferences	People seeking more organized or formal experiences had more specific requirements of the landscape (e.g. rock faces for climbing); people preferring a more informal experience were more likely to absorb the landscape in a more intuitive or organic way
Specialism	Whether people have a specialist interest or knowledge that they pursue outdoors

and membership of environmental organizations. For example, nature-connected users tended to be older, while nature sympathizers were younger; nature-connected users tended to be rural; and nature sympathizers and nature lovers were more likely to be members of environmental protection organizations. Amongst the authors' wider findings was confirmation of the point that attitudes that emerge in childhood tend to be retained and even reinforced in adulthood (c.f. van den Born et al., 2001).

Policy-oriented research (Natural England, 2009a) has identified a range of different attitude types amongst people, showing differing levels of integration or engagement with the landscape (Table 1.2). They ranged from those who were more transactional, seeing the landscape as a place to obtain exercise or entertainment, to those who considered the landscape to be part of the fabric of their lives either because they worked there or had deep-seated specialist interests. The research also found some differences in the way people experience the landscape according to demographic factors (their age, physical capabilities and gender), situational factors (such as the composition of their visiting group), their awareness or familiarity with the landscape, and their personal preferences (e.g. for structured or unstructured activity).

A great deal of literature on landscape has emphasised 'beauty', and the way that visual inputs can give pleasure to the mind. Landscape aesthetics persistently draws on ideas such as complexity, choice of colours, perspective and balance. This results in a 'visual aesthetic' in which landscape is presumed to give delight to the observer. The visual aesthetic has been a long-standing focus of landscape policy, so that measures to protect scenically important land have sought to minimize rates and degrees of unsympathetic change. This has evolved into policies that seek to reinforce strong visual character and reduce the visually chaotic consequences of intensive land development and management. We will note in due course how this visual aesthetic has been contrasted with the idea of an 'ecological aesthetic'. Thus, whilst some landscapes elicit aesthetic experiences that have traditionally been called 'scenic beauty', others elicit different aesthetic experiences, such as perceived care, attachment and identity. Hence, there is a possibility that we can develop, or perhaps reacquire, an ecological aesthetic that looks beyond the prettiness and tidiness of a landscape to detect cues about its underlying sustainability and resilience. In turn, we may have to move away from exercising fastidious care of urban green spaces and the preservation of rural prettiness in order to develop new ideas about caring for landscapes with non-classical beauty and a measure of environmental risk (Nassauer, 1997). Thus, reconnecting to landscapes means looking beyond the view, to understand the dynamics that are unseen but critical to social–ecological resilience, and perhaps to re-educate ourselves in a new ethic of landscape care.

Space and place

Geographers and planners often make a distinction between 'space' and 'place'. The former is concerned simply with the social and physical attributes of a location or area, and the role of actual or perceived distance. The notion of place relates more deeply to attributes that make a place special and distinct, and it often derives from the activities and experiences of people who live there. For example, Olwig (2008) refers to two different ways of seeing landscape. The first involves binocular vision, movement and knowledge gained from a coordinated use of the senses in carrying out various tasks on earth, fields, pastures, country and ground (Ingold, 1993). The second derives primarily from a monocular perspective that is fixed and distant from the body. Thus, the former engenders a sense of belonging that generates landscape as the place of 'dwelling and doing' – it might be thought of as the landscape of community. The latter constructs a feeling of possession and staged performance in which those who 'gaze' over the land are organized in a hierarchy of power – it might be thought of as the landscape of the colonist, proprietor, military surveyor, planner or even tourist. Olwig further suggests that the former has 'platial' qualities, comprising farms, fenced fields and regional polities (Mels, 2005); it is not so much a scenic surface as a woven material created through the merging of body and senses that occurs through 'dwelling'. The latter, by contrast, is 'spatial'; it is typified by the surveyor's orthogonal gaze, for example, as a basis for agricultural improvement.

Policy makers often suggest that people attach to places, and that it is desirable to protect and enhance the special qualities of places in ways that reinforce a sense of pride and belonging. The notion of 'power of place' was championed by English Heritage, stemming from the premise that 'the historic environment has the potential to strengthen the sense of community and provide a solid basis for neighbourhood renewal' (English Heritage, 2000, p. 23). Planners have often referred to the importance of place shaping, including the active involvement of people in defining the distinctive qualities of their place and in contributing to decisions that affect these qualities. Although the terms 'power of place' or 'place-shaping' rarely occur in official documents, there is widespread use of related terms such as community cohesion, citizenship, well-being, inclusive communities, community empowerment, identity and agency (Bradley et al., 2009).

In terms of urban design, the ancient term *genius loci* has latterly been reintroduced to refer to a sense of place associated with the physical and symbolic values in a locality (Jiven and Larkham, 2003). The Norwegian architect Christian Norberg-Schulz (1980) identified four ingredients that create a *genius loci*: the topography of the earth's surface; the cosmological light conditions and the sky; buildings; and symbolic and existential meanings in the cultural landscape. The notion of local character as produced through the sum of its parts has been used by academic disciplines linked to practice – for instance in urban design's concern with authenticity and its relationship with new developments, in marketing's focus on place branding, or the interest in 'place shaping' within public art projects (Graham et al., 2009). The key idea is that places can be shaped to encourage a more defined 'sense of place' with which people can more actively engage.

In a well known critique of such ideas, Massey (2005) noted that we tend to yearn for imagined pasts when places were supposedly inhabited by close-knit communities. She recognized our urge to preserve places that appeared to conform to this imagined past and criticized it as a reactionary, sentimentalized and defensive response through which we try to retrieve sanitized 'heritages'. Although Massey challenged many of the more uncritical assumptions about place and locality, she did conclude that distinctive locales do exist, to which people may display emotional attachment. However, the social composition of these places, and their absorption of non-local cultural influences, means that their character and composition are constantly changing. The subsequent discussions about place perhaps give greater emphasis to the physical characteristics of landscape, although it is important to be aware of Massey's social critique, and to avoid naive assumptions about the ways in which occupants of a locality identify with it.

Physical connections and the landscape: some preliminary terminology

Ecological connectivity

Biological conservation has, since the early part of the twentieth century, centred on the concept of ecosystems, and so has prioritized the protection of natural and semi-natural habitats. In places, there has been a particular interest in habitats that support charismatic or attractive animals and plants. Whilst this focus remains important, it has not proved wholly effective; biodiversity has continued to decline, principally due to trends on land outside protected areas.

More recent approaches to ecological management have aimed at overcoming the effects of isolation on protected areas. First, scientists have addressed the issue of optimum shape and size of reserves and other protected lands – if these are the wrong shape, they may be disproportionately damaged by 'edge effects' that cause disturbance of sensitive core areas, and if they are the wrong size they may be unable to support the feeding and life-cycle requirements of key species. Second, there has been a growing emphasis on joining up 'networks' of protected sites, either by improving the ways in which reserves complement each other over space (e.g. staging posts for migratory wildfowl) or by physically connecting habitats by linear corridors, which may in certain configurations assist population movements and the mixing of gene pools. Third, there has been a concern to promote wildlife friendly conditions in the wider matrix of land use, for example by making agricultural landscapes less monocultural so that they become more permeable and porous to wildlife movements. Finally, there has been a recent interest in building resilience in habitats and wildlife populations so that they have sufficient space and functionality to recover from major disturbances such as climate change.

Hydrological connectivity

Since around the seventeenth century, people have progressively applied new technologies to 'tame the flood' in order to permanently inhabit low-lying areas with high potential for agriculture and trade. Water tables have been systematically lowered and rivers straightened, whilst groundwater reserves have been exploited. As towns have spread, so rivers have been increasingly engineered, to be harnessed for industrial power or to stop flooding. Although rivers are still often valued and enjoyed, they are also often marginalized and even hidden, and wetlands have been extensively drained. Sometimes people are only aware that a river exists when it floods, leading to demands for it to be regulated and culverted even more. This has led to an 'engineered disconnection' (Wheater and Evans, 2009) between rivers and their natural floodplains.

The conventional 'grey infrastructure' – concrete, asphalt and steel – approach to floodplain management can only succeed within limits. Floodplains are, in principle, highly suitable for human habitation: they provide flat and fertile lands, access to drinking and industrial water, and good communications by land and water. In the first instance, conventional civil engineering may be a very effective way of enabling people to occupy floodplains safely and prosperously. Once development exceeds a certain level, however, recurrent problems occur. Buildings inevitably creep into the traditional floodplain as suitable development land becomes scarce; rivers and groundwaters become excessively polluted by domestic and industrial waste; the hardening of urban surfaces as they are 'sealed' by impermeable construction materials causes unnaturally rapid run-off; over-engineered stretches of river may simply cause flood hazards to be shifted from one location to another; and problems associated with groundwater can cause buildings to be attacked 'from below'. Further, the loss of natural functions in floodplains can reduce their resilience to adapt to changes in climate such as increasing frequency and intensity of rainfall events.

In response to these problems, new approaches seek to 'unseal' surfaces and reinstate connections between land, surface waters and groundwater in the functional floodplain. These approaches are broadly referred to as sustainable drainage systems (SuDS) – sometimes written as sustainable urban drainage systems (SUDS). SuDS cannot solve all flooding issues but offer many benefits compared with traditional systems, and they provide habitat creation as well as flood attenuation. Such approaches may also need to be coupled to highly participative styles of planning, so that social and institutional learning begins to occur in ways that enable people and organizations to live and work with new approaches that sometimes involve acceptance of increased levels of flood risk.

Green infrastructure

The term 'green infrastructure' has become increasingly popular as a planning concept (Natural England, 2009c). It encompasses ideas about ecological and hydrological connectivity, and a general reduction in reliance on grey infrastructure. It is usually, although not necessarily, applied to urban areas, and typically suggests that there is a natural resource base to the city, which, if sustainably managed and physically reconnected, can contribute in a multifaceted way to the amelioration of living conditions. It builds upon a long tradition of providing public open space, and represents the current evolution of thinking about ways in which green spaces in urban areas can best be provided and maintained in order to provide a range of public benefits. It is sometimes referred to as blue–green infrastructure, reflecting the importance of water circulation alongside green space, or as natural infrastructure, recognizing the additional significance of air and soil. It is viewed as being equivalent to the grey infrastructure of roads, sewers and so forth that provide an essential foundation for urban development. Green, unlike grey, infrastructure, however, cannot be hidden away underground, and it requires the active involvement of communities and landowners in its use and maintenance.

Active transport

The personal and environmental benefits of 'active transport' – walking, jogging, cycling, horse riding – have long been recognized, but the facility to practise them safely and enjoyably, especially in major towns, has been seriously curtailed by the spread of development and growth in traffic. Also, the possibility to take purposeful journeys – aimed at a destination such as the workplace rather than undertaken simply as a leisure outing – has been reduced by the haphazard nature of rights-of-way networks and the severance of through routes by development. In the open countryside, this has sometimes been addressed by the creation of long distance paths and cycle routes, and more ambitious 'greenway' networks. Opportunities for safe, continuous active transport in cities, however, have often been woefully deficient.

The creation of cycle lanes has been achieved with varying degrees of success in many cities. However, there is increased interest in the possibility of integrating active transport with multifunctional green infrastructure networks, where a far higher quality of experience can be achieved. Moreover, where these networks are genuinely multifunctional – for example, providing practical transport connections as well as a more general suite of environmental services – it will be easier to justify their funding and protection.

Town–country

Land use policy and planning has tended to show a sharp discontinuity between town and country. Land use changes in towns are predominantly controlled by spatial planning mechanisms whereas most rural land use change is exempt from planning control (although it is affected by subdivision control in some countries). Rural land use management is often strongly influenced by agricultural and forestry policy. Landscape planning in the country is often restrictive, focused on the protection of highly scenic areas. Landscape planning in urbanized and industrialized areas is often focused on the provision of urban green space and public realm, management of urban tree stocks, and regeneration of derelict land. Rivers in the countryside are often used for water supply and agricultural land drainage; urban rivers are often heavily engineered for flood control and waterfront economic activities. Between town and country, there is often a messy urban fringe and sprawling edge city, which acts neither as an effective bridge to the country nor a gateway to the town.

As cities have become cleaner and more focused on information and cultural activities, as rural areas have become more like towns in their economic activities and social composition, and as both increasingly share a common culture through the Internet and other globalizing trends, so the difference between town and country has become blurred. This creates a situation in which: we can no longer have unrealistic assumptions about preserving a 'picture postcard' countryside, but may need to accept new types of landscape, such as those associated with sustainable energy production; cities can expect to have a substantial green infrastructure, providing an accessible landscape that reduces the need for long-distance carbon-generating leisure trips; and the urban fringe might be promoted as a multifunctional space assisting continuity between airsheds, hydrological systems and ecological networks.

Conclusion

A study of landscape connections needs to draw upon multiple disciplines. It needs to assemble evidence from the arts and philosophy, from the social and behavioural sciences, as well as from the natural sciences and policy and design professions (Figure 1.3). Often these disciplines do not communicate very well with each other as they have very different knowledge bases and research methods. However, landscape requires holistic study, and so evidence from numerous fields must be synthesized if we are to understand the nature of disconnections and prospects for reconnection.

Before getting mired in complex explorations of landscape connectivity, it is useful at the outset to have a brief outline of the overall argument of the book. In essence, this book proposes that:

- physical landscape systems – such as ecosystems, rivers and microclimates – have, because of human pressures, become fragmented, damaged and disconnected;
- people are increasingly disconnected from the places in which they dwell, because they may work elsewhere, engage in 'virtual' worlds,

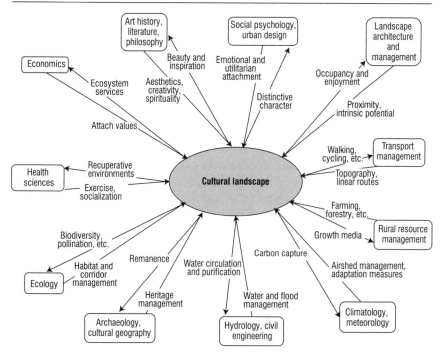

Figure 1.3 The cultural landscape as an integrative medium for multiple fields of knowledge

be drawn into global cultures, and rely on goods and services from distant origins;

- many landscapes have become less multifunctional than they used to be, and more mono-functional, possibly leading to a decline in resilience and visual interest;
- many natural scientists are concerned about the ways in which connections within and between environmental systems have been disrupted;
- some social scientists are concerned about the disruption of cultural and psychological factors that connect people to locality;
- people often appear to attach values to landscapes, and these values connect them to particular places and properties of nature;
- there is a diverse body of evidence from a range of disciplines that reveals the environmental, health and cultural benefits of restoring certain landscape connectivities;
- restoring connectivities will require action at various 'landscape scales' related to the innate dynamics of particular natural and social systems;
- certain natural functions will only reconnect if they are given sufficient space, whilst certain social functions may only reconnect if they are given distinctive place;

- if critical connectivities can be reinstated, the landscape will become more multifunctional – individual functions will be more readily sustained and they will interact synergistically in ways that make the whole more than the sum of the parts;
- landscapes that recover connections in this way may well prove to be more sustainable and resilient;
- if people have closer connections with the landscape itself, they are likely to make wiser choices that lead to a more resilient future;
- governance mechanisms should recognize the value of and opportunities for reinstating landscape connectivity.

Many of the desired qualities of cultural landscapes are 'emergent' – that is, they cannot simply be engineered or designed, but have to emerge spontaneously and unexpectedly. Complex, self-organizing systems need to be resilient and connected if these phenomena are to stand a chance of emerging serendipitously. The subsequent chapters explore the ways in which connections within the landscape can be understood and fostered, so that fortunate spontaneity and emergence might continue to occur.

Chapter 2

Functions, services and values of landscapes

Introduction

As noted in the previous chapter, an appreciation of landscape must go 'beyond the view'. The landscape we see is merely the surface manifestation of consolidated deposits of materials, practices and memories, and a dynamic regime of natural and societal systems. Human survival and well-being is reliant on these systems, yet there are concerns that their sustainability and resilience may have been compromised by progressive disconnection and disruption. Many authors have noted that landscape structures and systems deliver a range of functions, services and values (de Groot et al., 2002; de Groot, 2006; Haines-Young and Potschin, 2009; Willemen et al., 2010). However, these terms have been used ambiguously and inconsistently, and this chapter sets the scene by looking more closely at their meaning and significance.

Whilst landscape functionality is not obviously synonymous with landscape reconnection, in practice the two are closely related. It seems likely that landscapes that are sustainable and resilient will be those where robust functional connections exist within and between floodplains, ecological networks and other natural systems, and between natural and human systems. It is likely that they will supply a diverse range of ecosystem services. Further, for this type of functionality to be effective, it often needs to occur at a landscape scale (Selman, 2006), rather than being confined to isolated fragments, and thus relies upon having 'space' in which new equilibria can be established. It is then necessary for the physical to be linked to the social in order that landscape functions and services are valued, reinforced and maintained – this will tend to contribute to the emergence of 'place'.

When we simply look at the landscape with a detached gaze, we will see it as something instrumental, to be valued principally in terms of marketable commodities and enjoyable experiences. It has been argued that traditional cultures often value their land for its own sake and, out of reverence, do not exploit it selfishly. By contrast, industrial countries tend to 'asset strip' resources because of their utilitarian gaze on the environment and narrow interpretation of its market price rather than its broader value. Modern

---

Box 2.1 The key drivers of landscape change

Indirect drivers (examples)

- demographic changes;
- economic growth;
- sociopolitical changes, especially in policies;
- cultural and behavioural changes;
- advances in science and technology.

Direct drivers (examples)

- habitat change (particularly conversion of natural and semi-habitats through land use change or change in the use of the marine environment);
- nutrient enrichment and pollution of air, land and water;
- over-exploitation of terrestrial, marine and freshwater resources;
- variability and change in climate;
- introduction of invasive alien species.

---

economics increasingly takes account of the widespread existence of 'non-market' values in the landscape, and explores ways in which importance can be attributed to landscape functions and services. Such an approach, as was sought by the Millennium Ecosystem Assessment (2005), requires a social consensus to be built around the idea that, not only is a resilient and sustainable landscape important in its own right, but also such a landscape will have major benefits for human survival and prosperity. Thinking back to the previous chapter, such an attachment, either rational or emotional, is unlikely if there has been an 'extinction of experience'.

Human exploitation, which may sometimes be excessive and perhaps very indirect (such as the consequences of induced climate change), expresses itself as 'drivers' of landscape change. Conscious policy interventions by government, as well as a range of other practices by civil society, may seek to modify the intensity and direction of such changes. In this sense, they, too, are 'change drivers'. All landscapes are essentially dynamic, and constantly subject to change drivers, even where the rate of change is imperceptibly slow. These external forces are briefly summarized in Box 2.1.

This chapter sets out some core concepts relating to dynamic landscapes that are important for the subsequent exploration of landscape connection. The concepts relate to the basic functionality and service delivery of landscapes and also to the human and natural components of social–ecological systems.

Functions, services and values

The ways in which the functions of a landscape ultimately manifest themselves as values can be expressed as a cascade model (Figure 2.1) (Haines-Young and Potschin, 2009; Kienast et al., 2009). The landscape comprises stocks

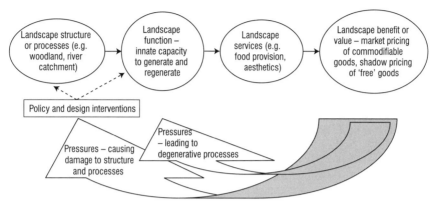

Figure 2.1 The cultural landscape as a system of structures, functions, services and values (adapted from Haines-Young and Potschin, 2009)

and flows of natural and cultural capital that underpin life and livelihood. These elements appear in the form of landscape structures (e.g. mountains, woodlands, cities) and ecosystem processes and functions (e.g. net primary productivity). Stocks and flows function in a way that supplies goods and services to the benefit of society. Outputs such as timber or food depend upon the landscape's capacity to supply the service and on society's demand for such a service. A landscape function is thus the intrinsic capacity of land to yield ecosystem services. The benefits that goods and services supply to society will possess values, and these may be reflected through the market (in which case their consumption may be more or less efficiently regulated), although their true worth may be seriously undervalued. Sometimes the value may not be recognized, because it has no commercial significance, and so the service may be taken for granted and unwittingly harmed. Where services are undervalued, then over-exploitation and disruption of underlying functions will tend to occur.

The key functions of landscape are those of regulation, habitat, production (or provisioning) and cultural (sometimes divided into information and carrier). As we will note, there is a strong link between these ecosystem services and human survival and well-being. Termorshuizen and Opdam (2009) have suggested that we might prefer to use the term 'landscape services' rather than ecosystem services, as this would include the notion of spatial organization, which is often integral to functionality. This view has considerable merit, as it is through the medium of landscape that services are drawn together and find spatial expression. However, the term 'ecosystem services' has gained very wide currency and for consistency is used here. Its most influential exposition has been the Millennium Ecosystem Assessment (MEA), sometimes referred to simply as the Millennium Assessment (MA), whose taxonomy of services has now widely been adopted as a basis for public policy (Figure 2.2).

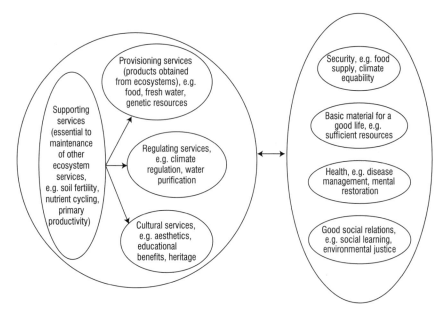

Figure 2.2 A taxonomy of ecosystem services (based on Millennium Ecosystem Assessment, 2005)

Functions are thus the fundamental capacities of landscape, whereas services and values are human derivatives of these. This book mainly addresses functions in order to explore the underlying properties and dynamics of landscape; it broadly assumes that stronger functionality will also more effectively and sustainably deliver services and generate higher landscape values. It also suggests that an essential and often emergent (i.e. unpredictable and serendipitous) quality of landscape is that it is more than the sum of its parts. Where functions are vibrant and interactive, they gain a synergy that produces a landscape that can be described as distinctive and multifunctional (Selman, 2009). It is important to bear in mind that services and values, important though they may be, do not necessarily add up to characteristic and resilient landscapes – it is the deeper functionality and connectivity of landscape that engenders the quality of emergence.

Contemporary economic pressures have led to many landscapes being concentrated on a small number of dominant functions in the pursuit of particular goods (e.g. cereals) or services (e.g. entertainment). Such landscapes may not have become entirely mono-functional, but they have become demonstrably less multifunctional. In more naturalistic, multifunctional landscapes, numerous different regulation, habitat, production, information and carrier functions are to be found in one place, and these interact synergistically in a dynamic system, with mutual reinforcement. As land use intensifies, natural cycles become disrupted by physical and chemical

Figure 2.3 Active management of woodland in the South Yorkshire Forest, UK, to promote multifunctional benefits of biodiversity, recreation, scenery, community engagement and sustainable fuel. The need to undertake such management often requires careful explanation and communication, otherwise site users may find it unacceptably intrusive

interventions, both intentional and accidental. Many landscapes have thus become more mono-functional, in the pursuit of increased productivity of desired goods and services. Such intensification is, of course, widely necessary, and Willemen et al.'s (2010) analysis of a rural landscape does indeed demonstrate how certain desired outputs (such as food production or touristic quality) may diminish as areas become less mono- and more multifunctional. However, even sites of intensive production are at risk of failure if they do not maintain a degree of multifunctionality, for example in relation to free services such as pollination. Landscape multifunctionality is therefore widely adopted as a desirable objective of land management and spatial planning; it requires that not only are multiple functions retained and enhanced within an area, but also that their synergy and interactivity are increased (Figure 2.3). This generally requires the maintenance or recovery of functional interconnectedness.

Based on an extensive review of the green space literature, Pauleit et al. (2003) found ample evidence of the values of natural green space in relation to amenity and recreation, reduction of pollution, moderation of the urban microclimate, and biodiversity. Recent discussions of this topic have tended to emphasize the importance not only of green space, but also of the need to link 'green' (e.g. grasslands, woodlands) with 'blue' (e.g. rivers, ponds). These can be combined into networks of increased functionality. As noted in the previous chapter, this is now commonly referred to as a 'green infrastructure', and is deemed to be as essential to the sustainability of towns as their grey infrastructure of roads and other conveyance systems. It also provides a mechanism for enhancing visual and functional continuity between urban and rural areas. One perspective on the nature and significance of landscape functions has been promoted by the Landscape Institute (2009) in the UK. They argued that the multifunctional nature of green infrastructure, underpinned by ecosystem services and enhanced through connectivity, can yield a diverse range of mutually reinforcing benefits (Box 2.2). All of these 'services' yield a range of landscape values, which can be quantified and given a social importance.

Landscape connectivities within 'nature'

As noted previously, the 'ecological' component of social–ecological systems is taken here to include a wide range of non-human resources and systems in the landscape, including hydrological, earth and atmospheric processes. The topic is addressed in greater detail in Chapter 4, but this section offers an initial review of key aspects of the functionality of landscape in relation to biodiversity support, biomass production, water catchments and air circulation (Figure 2.4).

The role of landscape in terms of biodiversity support is often related to physical connections between key habitats, and the way that ecosystem processes can operate at a landscape scale. The question of whether physical corridors in the landscape improve the prospects for biodiversity has been widely debated. As long ago as 1994, the topic was systematically reviewed by Dawson (1994) who synthesized the evidence about whether habitat corridors, such as hedgerows, offered a way of overcoming habitat fragmentation and barriers to dispersal. This supposed conduit function was based on concepts of metapopulation theory and landscape ecology, alongside other precursors such as island biogeography, home range and central place foraging theories. Dawson's conclusion was that the conduit function of corridors could not be substantiated by rigorously tested hypothesis-based evidence, and that there were alternative theories that might explain spatial patterns and processes. However, it did seem possible that some corridors were large enough in their own right to provide sufficient habitat for some species – indeed, they were sometimes the only remaining semi-natural habitat in an area – and that they may help to replenish some populations of animal and plant species and serve the needs of some migratory animals in their seasonal movements. It was doubtful whether good quality corridors could be found in sufficient quantity to allow sensitive species to move

Box 2.2 Services and benefits of green space (adapted from Landscape Institute, 2009)

- Adaptation to climate change – increases in tree canopy cover can help to reduce the urban heat island effect via evapotranspiration and shading, as well as improving air quality. A connected green infrastructure may help biodiversity respond to a changing climate, and ameliorate surface water run-off so as to reduce the risk of flooding.
- Mitigation of climate change – well designed and managed green infrastructure can encourage people to travel in more sustainable ways, such as cycling and walking. Trees can act as carbon sinks; trees and landform can reduce energy consumption in buildings associated with space heating and air conditioning, by providing shade in summer and shelter in winter. Landscape strategies can support the potential for efficient, decentralized, renewable energy, thereby improving local energy security.
- Flood risk management via sustainable drainage systems, and the use of agricultural and coastal land and wetlands to store flood water where it will do least damage to buildings. Measures involving wetland creation may also enhance carbon sequestration whilst providing important wildlife habitat.
- Waste assimilation, for example through the use of reed beds to remove pollutants from water, and through careful restoration of landfill sites to provide multifunctional after-uses.
- Food production, through its re-extension back into cities, creating space through allotments, community gardens and orchards; additional services are associated with increased access to healthy food, educational opportunities and food security, as well as the benefits of reconnecting communities with their local environment.
- Sustainable transport, connecting local communities via footpaths and cycleways. Connected, accessible landscapes also provide important opportunities for informal and active recreation, close to people's homes, with additional opportunities for social connection by involving people in the design and management of recreational spaces.
- Wildlife in both urban and rural areas, with the potential for taking a landscape-scale approach to the planning, design and management of habitats and habitat networks, increasing species' options for movement in response to environmental stress.
- Economic enhancement, associated with high quality green space that impacts positively on land and property markets, helps to create a setting for investment and acts as a catalyst for wider regeneration.
- Promoting a sense of place and fostering community spirit, especially where landscape enhancements engage local communities, and relate to landscape character and heritage.
- Education, both formal – providing an outdoor 'classroom' – and informal – helping people learn about their natural environment, which is a fundamental prerequisite of living within environmental limits.

in response to external pressures such as global warming. The idea that a network of small corridors enables large-scale movement was attractive but untested. Nonetheless, it was suggested that corridors should be enhanced as a 'precautionary principle' where feasible and cost-effective.

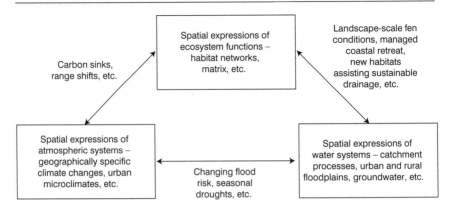

Figure 2.4 Principal physical systems and their spatial linkages within the landscape

Although quite a lot of new evidence has emerged about habitat networks since then, Dawson's conclusions remain broadly valid. The argument now tends to be more generally cast as 'making space for nature'. In other words, nature mainly needs higher quality habitat and a more permeable landscape structure that creates 'space' for species to extend and, if necessary, adjust their range in response to changing environmental conditions. This issue is explored further in Chapter 4.

A further key function of landscape-scale environmental processes is that of 'regulation', or the way that potentially harmful state changes can be buffered by natural regulators in environmental systems. Systems can be modelled in terms of 'driver–response' processes – for example, increased atmospheric carbon loadings could drive a response of rising temperature. The rate and intensity of these processes are regulated by the properties of the environmental subsystems. Thus, the landscape performs many 'regulating' functions – that is, its many subsystems are regulators of the speed and characteristics of driver–response processes. For example, when intense rainfall occurs and naturally moves across the floodplain towards a river, the vegetation, soil and near-surface permeable rocks will slow down the rate of movement and perhaps return some of the moisture to deep groundwater or the atmosphere, or use it for plant growth. The floodplain is thus a natural regulator. However, this function may be diminished if, for example, hard urban surfaces seal the natural ground cover or highly efficient field drains accelerate run-off from farmland.

Another key regulation function relates to the amount of carbon in the atmosphere. Both soil and vegetation, as well as marine organisms, have varying capacities to take up and store atmospheric carbon. Recent years have witnessed a growing concern that, not only have atmospheric carbon levels greatly increased, but also the natural regulators such as tree cover have diminished. There is currently a great deal of concern about the global reduction in the biosequestration capacity of soils, particularly from agricultural soils and dry lands (Trumper et al., 2009). Whilst there are still many uncertainties about the amounts sequestered under different management regimes, and the sequestration capacity of different areas and soil types, there is a strong case for promoting conservation and restoration measures.

Many forecasts have been made about future climate. It should be borne in mind that these are not intended to be accurate predictions, and their outcomes are often misused and taken too literally by the popular media. Instead they should be seen as evidence-based scenarios that can alert us to a range of contingencies so that we can start to map out future unknowns and anticipate possible responses. As an illustration of these forecasts, UK Climate Projections (Jenkins et al., 2009) have been produced to provide a probabilistic estimate of future climate based on high, medium and low emission scenarios. Results are generally provided in terms of central estimates of change (50 per cent probability level), as well as those levels of changes that are very likely to be exceeded (10 per cent probability level) and those very likely not to be exceeded (90 per cent probability level). In the following summary, the 50 per cent level is given, followed by the 10 per cent and 90 per cent range in brackets. Changes predicted to occur by the 2080s, relative to a 1961–1990 baseline, are that all areas of the UK become warmer, especially in terms of summer temperatures. Changes in summer mean temperatures are greatest in parts of southern England, where they may be up to +4.2°C (2.2–6.8°C) and least in the Scottish islands at just over +2.5°C (1.2–4.1°C). Mean daily maximum temperatures increase everywhere. Increases in the summer average are up to 5.4°C (2.2–9.5°C) in parts of southern England and 2.8°C (1–5°C) in parts of northern Britain. Central estimates of annual precipitation amounts show little change at the 50 per cent probability level. The biggest increases in winter precipitation (up to about 33 per cent) are seen along the western side of the UK, whilst the biggest decreases in summer (around 40 per cent) are seen in parts of the far south of England. There are increases in the number of ten-day dry spells across the UK, and these are more pronounced in southern England and in Wales.

Ecological forecasts suggest that a number of native species are likely to lose 'climate space' as a consequence of these changes. For example, in relation to trees, the geographical ranges of many species will shift, suggesting that they will struggle on many sites, their regeneration and successful establishment will decline and they could be out-competed by introduced species from more southerly regions that are better suited to new climatic conditions. The distribution of tree species will inevitably change in response to climate warming. However, if the trees are to stay within appropriate climatic envelopes it has been suggested that species migration rates will need to be more than ten times faster than those achieved in reaching present distributions after the last ice age (Broadmeadow et al., 2009).

Box 2.3 Estimated climatic services of wooded landscapes

One study in the UK examined the possibility of significantly increasing the rate of new planting (to around 23 000 hectares (ha) a year from the actual 8 360 ha per year). The results suggested that:

- by the 2050s this could, in combination with the maturation of woodland planted since 1990, effectively abate around 10 per cent of total GHG emissions;
- the most cost-effective options appeared to be conifer plantations and rapidly growing energy crops, but mixed woodlands managed for multiple objectives could also deliver highly cost-effective abatement;
- if no action was taken to significantly increase the rate of woodland creation, the rate of atmospheric CO_2 uptake by forests in the UK would decline from a maximum of 16 million tonnes (Mt) of CO_2 per year in 2004 to 4.6 $MtCO_2$ per year by 2020;
- these declines would be associated with forest age structure, the maturation and harvesting of the woodlands created as a result of the afforestation programmes of the 1950s to 1980s, and the decline in planting rates since the 1980s;
- existing UK forests, including soils, are both a large store of carbon (estimated at around 790 $MtCO_2$) and a system removing CO_2 from the atmosphere;
- sustainable forest management can maintain the carbon store of a forest at a constant level while the trees continue to remove CO_2 from the atmosphere and transfer a proportion of the carbon into long-term storage in forest products;
- total carbon stored in the forest and its associated 'wood chain' therefore increases over time under appropriate management systems. This contribution could be increased further if bioenergy was used for heating, including energy derived from woody biomass, as this provides one of the most cost-effective and environmentally acceptable ways of decreasing GHG emissions. Using timber in construction also locks in carbon (Read et al., 2009).

The climate regulation function of landscape is often related to its tree cover (Box 2.3). An influential report on the role of forests in combating climate change (Read et al., 2009) noted that forests remove carbon dioxide (CO_2) from the atmosphere through photosynthesis and, globally, could provide abatement equivalent to about 25 per cent of current CO_2 emissions from fossil fuels by 2030, through a combination of reduced deforestation, forest management and afforestation. Woodland creation proves to be a very cost-effective approach to greenhouse gas (GHG) abatement relative to other options. Woodlands and forests are a net sink of CO_2 and, except during tree harvesting and for a relatively short period thereafter, they remove CO_2 from the atmosphere. Whilst there will be an upper limit to which forest carbon stocks will be a 'sink' for carbon, total abatement can continue to rise over successive rotations because of carbon storage in wood products and the substitution of wood for fossil fuel. It would appear that some of the more intensive alternatives for managing forests – those that are more selective and less mechanized – may have significantly improved rates of carbon sequestration.

As well as mitigation potential, trees also have important adaptation potential, particularly in the urban environment, through providing shelter, cooling, shade and run-off control. This is considered later in relation to urban climate.

A further crucial regulation function is that of water balance (Wheater and Evans, 2009). Again, the climate change driver will be central, especially because of the anticipated changes in precipitation. Although future precipitation is highly uncertain, increased frequency of extreme events is expected, and this is likely to exacerbate different types of flooding. Kondolf et al. (2006), studying lost river linkages, noted how human impacts on aquatic ecosystems often involve changes in hydrological connectivity and flow regime. Hydrological connectivity refers to water-mediated transfers of matter, energy, and organisms within or between the river channel, floodplain, aquifer and other components. This hydrologic connectivity can be viewed as operating in longitudinal, lateral and vertical dimensions and over time. Kondolf et al. reported how broadscale theories of river ecosystem connectivity initially focused on longitudinal gradients but progressively broadened out to include the lateral linkages with the floodplain, the riparian zone and the vertical connection with groundwater. Our understanding of how the longitudinal, lateral and vertical dimensions work together is relatively recent, as is our appreciation of the critically important effects of loss of connectivity between these elements. Wohl (2004) has systematically shown how human activities have impoverished rivers and impaired the connections between river systems and other ecosystems. It is now acknowledged that longitudinal, lateral and vertical vectors of hydrological connectivity underpin nearly all ecosystem processes and patterns in rivers, at multiple scales, and that disconnection explains much of the ecological degradation of rivers. A wide range of human interventions, from levee construction to channel deepening, may meet the immediate need to control certain magnitudes of flows but will also reduce other important floodplain processes. For example, restrictions to lateral connectivity will decrease floodplain productivity, nutrient exchange, and dispersal of biota between the river and floodplain wetlands (Jenkins and Boulton, 2003).

Engineers and planners will face serious problems in the relatively near future if we need to find the space in riverside towns and cities to accommodate significantly increased flood events. This is because urban planning policy has strongly promoted the reuse of brownfield sites. Although there is a strong sustainability case for the reuse of brownfield sites, there has always been a concern that it could result in 'town cramming', removing space for essential ecosystem services. Potentially, therefore, this intensive use of land and loss of open space could increase problems of urban flooding, particularly where regeneration measures have focused on urban waterfronts (Wheater and Evans, 2009).

Urbanization acts as a driver of flood risk by increasing the assets at risk of flooding, and by increasing run-off, which in turn creates potential hazards for downstream areas. However, this issue is not a simple one: as Evans et al. (2004) note, it would be difficult to ban redevelopment of brownfield sites that lie in the floodplain, but which are behind well managed flood defences. A more resilient approach may include the renewal of existing urban spaces, new urban forms, new densities of development and more green space. However, there is actually relatively little opportunity to create genuinely new and resilient urban forms according to principles of sustainable design, not least because a typical rate at which new housing is added to the overall housing stock in developed countries is only around 1 per cent per annum. Of greater importance, therefore, will be the way that resilience can be retrofitted into existing fabric, for example through sustainable drainage systems and source controls.

In rural areas, increased flooding will affect agricultural land and productivity. Rural land is both a driver of flood risk and a receptor. It is thought that rural land use intensification has increased run-off generation at the local and small catchment scales, compounded in many places by soil degradation. Even so, agricultural land can also help to mitigate flood risk, both by reducing run-off generation, and by using some agricultural floodplain land for flood storage and attenuation. Washlands such as these are also multifunctional, and they have benefits for diffuse pollution mitigation as well as for wildlife habitats. In peri-urban areas agricultural intensification, together with additional urbanization, has produced significant changes in the volumes of run-off entering the urban area, including the effects of reduced infiltration and increased overland flow. Although flooding and soil waterlogging can clearly cause loss and distress, especially in more intensively farmed areas, generally farmland is more tolerant of flooding than urban land, and has lower unit costs of damage. Hence there is growing interest in 'setting back' some previous agricultural flood defences to allow increased flooding and restore natural floodplains in ways that provide benefits in terms of both flood storage and biodiversity. Such measures, of course, impose distress and financial risks on farmers and so society needs to compensate for this in appropriate ways (Wheater and Evans, 2009).

Inundation is also a threat at the coast because of rising sea levels and tidal surges, combined with the fact that some coastlines are sinking. There has been a lot of research and several practical projects relating to the managed realignment of the coastline, in which the sea is allowed to inundate land that has previously been reclaimed for permanent agriculture from habitats such as saltmarshes. This is seen as an increasingly viable solution to coastal flood and erosion defence problems in many areas. However, whilst the land lost to the sea through managed retreat is only a tiny fraction of total agricultural land, often the areas that depend highly on flood protection and land drainage are a significant proportion of the most agriculturally productive land (Evans et al., 2004). There is therefore a potential conflict between the long-term management of marine inundation and food production.

Urban areas typically experience a 'heat island' effect relative to the surrounding countryside, due to their dominance by hard surfaces that store more heat, which is then slowly released. The effect is compounded by the high incidence of reflective surfaces such as glass, as these reflect radiation between surfaces that would normally be emitted into the atmosphere. The heat island effect is intensified by transport, space heating and cooling systems, and industrial activities. This means that cities may be several degrees warmer than adjacent rural areas, and the result can be very oppressive during hot summers. Gill et al. (2007) report that the urban environment has distinctive biophysical features in relation to surrounding rural areas. These include an altered energy exchange creating an urban heat island, and changes to hydrology such as increased surface run-off of rainwater. Such changes are, in part, a result of the altered surface cover of the urban area. For example reducing vegetated cover leads to a decrease in evaporative cooling, whilst an increase in surface sealing results in increased surface run-off. These effects will be exacerbated by climate change.

Landscape connectivities within 'society'

This section sets the scene in relation to the social functions of landscape before connections are looked at in greater detail in Chapter 5. As noted previously, the 'social' of social–ecological systems needs to be interpreted broadly, to include issues relating to individuals, society, community, economy, culture and governance. In particular, this section centres on core concepts of social capital and human well-being that are critical to understanding the potentials and functions of reconnected landscapes.

The notion of social capital refers to benefits that are generated through interactions between people. It can manifest itself in a diversity of groupings, including communities-of-place (specific localities), communities-of-interest (groupings that centre on a shared interest amongst a network of people), and communities-of-practice (groups of stakeholders who work towards a collective purpose). It is often suggested that there can be a close connection between social capital networks and the locality in which they operate – this is what most people understand simply as 'community'.

Social capital generally refers to the networks of friendship, trust, mutual assistance and civic engagement that exist in communities of various types. On the one hand, it has a cultural meaning, popularized by Pierre Bourdieu's ideas about the ways in which differentiation and inequality in society are preserved through social interactions (Bourdieu, 1997, pp. 51–53) – often caricatured as 'who you know rather than what you know'. On the other hand, it has a more sociological meaning, as championed by the American sociologist Robert Putnam. The latter has been described as a more policy friendly term and is more pertinent to the current discussion. It emphasizes how social capital can be generated for all social groups through exchanges that occur within community and friendship networks. For Putnam, the extent and type of interactions can provide individuals with access to a range of benefits such as well-being, good health and civic engagement. Importantly for landscape, Graham et al. (2009) point out that whilst Putnam does not have a particular focus on 'place', it is clear that he imagines a range of free and accessible spaces within which social capital interactions might take place.

Putnam (2000) refers to two types of social capital: bonding and bridging. The former tends to be exclusionary, making it difficult for incomers to be accepted within close-knit groups, whilst the latter tends to be more inclusive of new entrants so that it links groups. Bonding capital serves to create bonds between people who have been closely associated over a long time with a particular place or industry, and may therefore display very strong signs of community and mutual interdependence. However, such communities may sometimes be hostile to outsiders or to individuals who are in some sense 'other' (e.g. because of their colour, religion or sexual orientation). Bridging capital refers to the connections between people in ways that often make bridges between groups and individuals that would otherwise have had little in common and would have remained dissimilar and separate. Although less obviously geographically centred than bonding capital, bridging capital may be quite strongly associated with place and can operate powerfully amongst people living in a local community. Some writers also refer to 'linking' capital (although others consider it to be a subset of bridging capital), which is similar but tends to operate through organizations that may be relatively unrelated to locality. Bonding capital is often associated with traditional, stable communities, often closely related to place-specific modes of employment such as coal mining. It is often reflected in socializing, and local and community level participation. Lewicka (2005) has explored the apparent paradox of a positive link between place attachment and civic activity, and the seemingly contradictory argument that place attachment declines as a person's social and cultural status (cultural capital) increases. One explanation may be that, whilst the more mobile middle classes tend to display relatively low bonding capital, they may possess greater reserves of bridging/linking capital associated with more formal civil participation, which may reflect a desire to create social networks through active involvement in organizations.

Whilst social capital is generally considered to be good and necessary, bonding social capital can run the risk of a 'tyranny of community', accepting only those types of person who fit in. Indeed, some have suggested that loss of community may be the price we pay for a more tolerant society. Some writers have emphasized the role of social relations that define 'place', and these may reinforce the internal relations of power and inequality whilst excluding the 'other'. Hence, newcomers who are enrolled into local social networks may be expected to adhere to its norms and conventions, reproducing the distinctions between those who are accepted or 'inside' and those who are not. However, the counter-argument to these rather negative views is that community spirit and inclusiveness are not incompatible. Notably, Putnam presents evidence to the effect that social capital is reinforcing, and those that reach out to friends and family are often also the most active in community outreach (Putnam, 2000). Generally speaking, most of the discussion about social capital in relation to landscape tends to assume that it is a self-evident good. Clearly, this is not always the case: not only may social capital lead to exclusion and rejection, but also some antisocial organizations, such as gangs, can display high levels of mutual trust, support and loyalty that are the hallmarks of social capital. Nevertheless, 'good' social capital reinforces reciprocity and trust within communities, and this is widely taken as a prerequisite for social sustainability and resilience, and for people's relationship to place.

Further, an adaptive and resilient society will be capable of 'social learning'. Often, it has been assumed that community stakeholders do not understand the science underlying environmental issues, and so need to have their 'knowledge deficit' plugged by experts, who tell them about the nature of the issue and the solutions that must be accepted in order to fix the problem (Petts, 2006). However, where new and complex issues are being faced, and innovative solutions being explored, there is a need to gain widespread acceptance of proposed responses and their associated risks, based on a broad understanding of the challenge being faced. In these situations, it has been argued that institutions and communities need to come together in order to explore new ways of solving shared problems. By combining expert knowledge and analysis with local experience and wisdom, it may increase the possibility of bringing about changes that are effective and acceptable because they have been based on a broad platform of evidence, experience and mutual respect. It has been suggested that social learning can support an evolving understanding of problems, opportunities, organizational partnerships, research requirements and actions. In later chapters, we will consider the ways in which social learning can occur in landscape settings, and contribute to the production of a multifunctional, adaptive, resilient landscape.

Brummel et al. (2010) have promoted communicative learning; namely, learning about values and intentions, learning how to work together and building a common identity. This approach draws upon the notion of transformative learning (Mezirow, 1997) that posits ways in which people find more integrated, sustainable solutions to difficult problems. Such an approach may not be appropriate to debating specific landscape management interventions, but may be invaluable for developing a broader base of shared understanding. Muro and Jeffrey (2008) noted how

Milbrath (1989) linked social learning to sustainable development using the expression 'self educating' community to describe circumstances where people learn from each other and from nature. They observe that early accounts of social learning focused on cognition, in other words the ways that factual understanding was developed and refined through learning with others, through feedback and reciprocity between the learners. However, this is now seen as too narrow to embrace all the learning processes that are relevant to participatory and sustainable landscape management. More recent explorations of social learning have tended to view participation and deliberation as mechanisms to create different forms of rationality and civic virtue that together can form the basis for better environmental decisions. Through taking this 'situated' approach to learning, people can develop an understanding of inter-subjective perceptions and tensions between stakeholders, and this may be especially relevant to solving the intractable problems associated with sustainable development. It may also bring about transformative learning, in which people gradually change their views on themselves and the world, and thus become more able to identify and accept changes in their lifestyles and circumstances.

Keen et al. (2005) note that, in relation to environmental issues, social learning draws together three principal partners – community, specialists and government – with the intention of producing both knowledge and ethics that support collective action towards a sustainable future. Several techniques may be used for this but, at the heart of them, is the need to engender a reflective process. Reflexivity in environmental management is an important lever for social change because it can reveal how theoretical, cultural, institutional and political contexts affect our learning processes, actions and values (Figure 2.5). To reflect on ourselves and our practices, we need catalysts that can help us see what would otherwise be invisible to us. Similarly, Petts (2006) identifies the key elements of social learning as comprising recruitment of representative interests, active facilitation, collaborative framing, optimizing interaction and managing the unexpected. Both public and expert can learn if the right conditions for listening, sharing, reflecting on preferences and adapting are present. Tippett (2004) suggests that participants need to 'think like an ecosystem' searching for ways of ensuring that the landscape system has sufficient diversity to give it resilience, or the ability to react to change. As an integral part of this system, stakeholders and practitioners need to develop the capacity to meet future challenges.

Perhaps the pre-eminent 'cultural' service afforded by landscape is its potential to contribute to physical, mental and spiritual health (Morris, 2003). As already noted, the concept of a 'restorative environment' implies that the landscape can provide an environment that enhances the recovery of mental energies and effectiveness. In addition, a spatially well connected landscape will also create important opportunities for fitness and exercise.

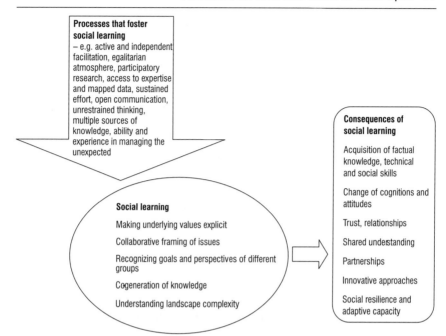

Figure 2.5 The nature and benefits of social learning (based on Muro and Jeffrey, 2008)

Given the more sedentary lifestyles of technologically developed nations, and the way in which walking has changed from being a routine mode of transport to a leisure pursuit, it is important to encourage higher levels of physical activity. Outdoor activity also increases opportunities for social interaction, with attendant benefits for well-being.

The notion of 'well-being' is widely used in relation to the benefits of green spaces, with some researchers claiming that the natural environment provides synergistic physical, mental and social well-being benefits. However, there are problems with gathering acceptable evidence on the topic, as many of those interested in it are from the medical professions, and yet much of the research is undertaken in academic subjects that do not meet these professions' requirements for robust clinical and quantitative evidence. Further, there is no single agreed definition of well-being: it is a broad and contested term, incorporating objective and measurable dimensions such as level of wealth and provision of education and health care, as well as subjective dimensions that seek to capture what individuals think and feel about their own circumstances.

Morris notes that much of the academic literature distinguishes between hedonic and eudaemonic approaches, and these debates have strongly influenced attempts to measure well-being. 'Hedonic psychology' entails the study of what makes experiences and life pleasant and unpleasant, focusing largely on the preferences and pleasures of the mind and body, and this perspective has been particularly influential on attempts to develop quantitative measures. Most research in this strand has drawn on the concept of 'subjective well-being', which consists of three components – life satisfaction, presence of positive mood, and absence of negative mood – often collectively referred to as 'happiness'. Eudaemonic theorists tend to give greater emphasis to 'psychological well-being'. They argue that 'happiness' is too narrow a criterion, as not all our pleasure-seeking desires will contribute to well-being and may even cause harm. It incorporates the idea that well-being is about achieving a sense of purpose and meaning in life – 'self-realization' – rather than pursuing pleasure. Self-determination theory (Ryan and Deci, 2000) proposes that this is achieved through the satisfaction of three psychological needs: autonomy (having a sense of control over one's life), competence (a sense that one is functioning effectively) and relatedness (having positive interactions with others). Both subjective and eudaemonic ideas have been of interest to government but the balance is now perhaps tipping towards the latter – the broader conception of well-being is seen to relate to a number of circumstances that lie within governmental influence.

Vuorinen (1990) has drawn attention to the concept of self-regulation, which refers to mental activity through which people process the psychological influences of outside factors. Self-regulation, and the closely related capacity for emotion regulation, enables an individual to function adaptively in situations that may otherwise be unbearably stressful. Vuorinen argues that people produce adaptive solutions to such situations by simultaneously operating two principles – self-determination and constancy. Thus, the individual strives to manage psychic tension by defining their self-experience in terms of images, cognitions and fantasies that they consider to be in their own power and control. Within the limits of the prevailing situation, a person tries to produce coherent and maximally beneficial consequences for self-experience and self-esteem. Epstein (1991) has offered a similar view of self-regulation, based on the idea that we develop a preconscious theory of reality and self. At the overarching level are basic beliefs about the world and human nature, whilst at progressively lower levels, these beliefs become narrower in scope and more closely associated with direct experience. It is generally agreed that these beliefs are not developed for their own sake but to make life as liveable, meaningful and emotionally satisfying as possible.

Importantly, in relation to our connections with landscape, it seems that our experience of places can be pivotal to our self-regulative functions, and so contribute to personal restoration. This is because ecosystem services may be associated with people's experiences and understandings that occur in particular places, especially familiar ones, and these may help people to regulate their emotional balance and self-experience (Korpela, 1989; Korpela et al., 2001).

A final main area of society–landscape connection lies in the economic processes that affect the functioning of 'nature'. Historically, many important cultural landscapes have effectively been the product of local economies coupled with the particularities of place. In contemporary culture, it could be argued that economic forces (predominantly exogenous ones) are widely reducing the multifunctionality and distinctiveness that were produced by previous – slower and more locally embedded – economic processes. Essentially, the distinctiveness of large-scale landscape can be produced or maintained in one of three ways:

1 by a natural and serendipitous linkage of social and economic drivers to physical landscape so that productive practices spontaneously produce landscapes of character;
2 by taxpayer contributions to the maintenance of ecologically resilient management practices (often based on traditional approaches that are no longer economically viable without supplementary payments); or
3 by finding new sources of private income to maintain the appearance (but not necessarily the functionality) of characteristic aspects of the built and natural environment.

If we are seeking to enable the continued emergence of new expressions of landscape, there are clear benefits in coupling economic practices to the production of landscape character, as instanced in option '1' above. This may sometimes centre on traditional crafts and foods, for example, but may also be achieved by new drivers such as well planned volume housing or sustainable drainage systems.

Many landscapes have been caught in a vicious circle of decline, where agricultural abandonment or urban–industrial intensification have combined with wider social processes such as depopulation or dis-embedded local economic activity, so that landscapes lose character, distinctiveness and multifunctionality, and have no spontaneous mechanism for regeneration. It has been suggested that it is possible to engender a virtuous circle in which landscape quality is beneficial to local economy and quality of life, and where economic and social practices therefore find it beneficial to nurture landscape qualities (Selman, 2007; Selman and Knight, 2006)) (Figure 2.6).

In advanced industrial and post-industrial economies, virtuous circles in agricultural landscapes often need some kind of state subvention. Taxpayer support for particular types of farming may appear to be subsidizing inefficient and outdated practices. In reality, it often reflects the fact that, although many important landscape services (such as pollination and water regulation) are very valuable, they have no market value and hence no price. In such a situation of market failure, payments from general taxation for ecosystem services can therefore be justified. In addition, many valued traditional landscape features were the outcome of benign patronage; they were consciously planned as amenities by influential landowners. In contemporary society, non-governmental organizations (NGOs) and public

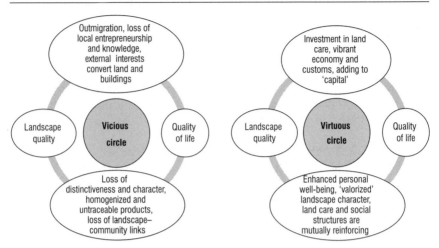

Figure 2.6 Vicious and virtuous circles in the landscape

bodies can legitimately play a similar role. Thus, social and governmental practices – such as 'friends of' groups or tax incentives – may mirror earlier modes of patronage and help to sustain preferred landscapes.

Conclusion

This chapter has introduced some key concepts underlying social and natural landscape systems that will be explored in greater detail in subsequent chapters. Landscape is now understood as a multifunctional and dynamic system that, through its natural and cultural layers, delivers a range of ecosystem services. These services are cultural as well as physical and biological, and all contribute to human well-being. It seems likely that humans have a fundamental need to experience 'nature' within their lives. This is in addition to the basic 'life support' role of ecological, hydrological and atmospheric systems. In a multifunctional landscape, there are well embedded connections between these systems (Figure 2.7). However, it would seem that the functionality of these systems is widely being undermined by loss of connectedness.

Some of the connections are predominantly human and social. Loss of connection to nature, both in childhood and adulthood, can reduce quality of life and may contribute to psychological distress. It may also adversely affect the persistence of social capital and, in turn, diminish our shared capacity to respond to environmental crises. It may reduce the basis for sustainable economic growth. Fragmentation of green corridors may also undermine the likelihood of a shift towards more sustainable transport patterns.

Some of the connections are principally within and between natural systems. Hydrological systems have been disrupted through the impact of urbanization and our attempts to control flooding. Certain changes in rural

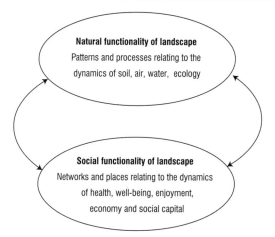

Figure 2.7 Broad linkages between natural and social landscape systems

land use are also interrupting the dynamics of systems that were previously capable of self-regulation. Atmospheric systems are changing because of the disruption of air paths and microclimatic zones within cities, and because of inadequate attention to the nature and structure of vegetation. Ecological resources are widely deteriorating due to loss of network properties. All of these diminish the capacity of 'nature' to deliver ecosystem services and to recover from disturbance.

Re-establishing lost linkages within and between natural and human systems may improve our well-being and increase our capacity to withstand future shock. It is suggested that the link between people and landscape has often behaved as a vicious circle of declining care and reduced quality. There is a possibility, therefore, that a well connected and multifunctional landscape will express a display of virtuosity, whereby people invest in landscapes because they see a link to enhanced ecosystem services, whilst the landscape in turn becomes more distinctive and adaptive. This principle of virtuosity underpins much of the subsequent argument concerning active reconnection.

Chapter 3

Change and resilience in landscapes

Change in cultural landscapes

Landscape is a dynamic system, not a static stage set. Some landscapes are 'fast change', for example where there are intense development pressures or where there is a reclamation programme for industrially damaged land. Some landscapes are 'slow change' and their visual impression of change may be restricted to seasonal colours; even so, they are still gradually and imperceptibly being altered by human and natural drivers. An awareness of the inexorability of change in all landscapes is fundamental to the ways in which we seek to inhabit, manage, design and plan them.

The popular view of landscape is that it is timeless, rooted firmly against human turmoil and transience. In reality, although the basic landform is essentially fixed, the cultural landscape is in constant flux. Natural change drivers include physical and ecological processes, some of which, such as carbon-forced increase in temperature, are now amplified by human activity (Winn et al., 2011). Cultural drivers include economic activity, social expectations about the use of land, and public policy. Landscape change is normal and ubiquitous, and some of it would occur in the absence of humans.

As a broad generalization, the kinds of landscapes most valued by humans are slow change landscapes in which change drivers are compatible with the innate capacities of local environmental systems and the persistence of material culture, and where social capital and economic entrepreneurship are embedded in the land and settlements. Where these conditions occur, it is generally the case that landscape change is sufficiently slow and subtle to ensure the retention of distinctive character. We often seek to conserve and protect slow change landscapes in order to reduce the rate of change of their valued attributes even further. It is often claimed that slow change landscapes will tend to be relatively multifunctional, that their stocks of natural and social capital will be aggrading rather than degrading, and that they will be comparatively resilient to future shocks. Such assumptions may often be justified.

Increasingly, we are starting to realize that, not only is protection by itself an inadequate basis for landscape policy, but also that slow change landscapes must not be overprotected and must be allowed to evolve. Recognizing the insufficiency of backward-looking conservation, Adams (2003) has advocated the complementary need to make space for 'future nature'. Thus, rather than solely trying to recapture and recreate cultural ecosystems of past agricultural economies, conservationists ought also to pay attention to the capacity of nature to regain ground in a future landscape. Outcomes would not be identical to the inherited habitats that dominate current conservation policy, since social systems, climatic conditions and other drivers of biodiversity change would be associated with a degree of unpredictability; instead, a 'future nature' would emerge, in some respects unfamiliar but in balance with ambient environmental and cultural conditions. This principle can be extended from biodiversity, and be applied to the wider evolution of a 'future landscape'.

However, this does not mean that the past becomes unimportant and that external, non-local change drivers should be uncritically welcomed. Another quality of landscape is that of 'remanence' (Le Dû-Blayo, 2011) – a term technically applied to residual magnetism in a metal after the magnet has been taken away, or to residual traces of erased data on an electronic storage medium. Landscape retains traces from all its previous stages and because these manifold influences in particular locations combine in unique ways, they confer specificity on the landscape. The analogy of a palimpsest document, on which previous scripts, erased and overwritten, can still faintly be detected, is often used to describe this phenomenon. Traces can be material, inscribed on the land by human labour or geomorphic processes, or intangible, in the form of memories, beliefs, customs and stories. Traces may be readily visible or only faintly sensed. Once material traces are obliterated, past wildlife populations extinguished or tales forgotten, the landscape is impoverished of its 'information' service and often does not retain the kind of complexity necessary for human well-being and cognitive development.

In the following discussions of landscape it is essential to appreciate the extent of change that occurs, even though we may want to ensure remanence. Even the most apparently stable and timeless landscape is being driven into a different state by natural and human factors. Distinctive and resilient landscape cannot therefore be secured by protection alone – the pursuit of reconnection needs to acknowledge that all landscapes are dynamic.

Change in the landscape can be understood in terms of the widely used DPSIR model, which supplies a causal framework for describing the interactions between society and the environment. The components of this model are:

- Driving forces
- Pressures
- States
- Impacts
- Responses

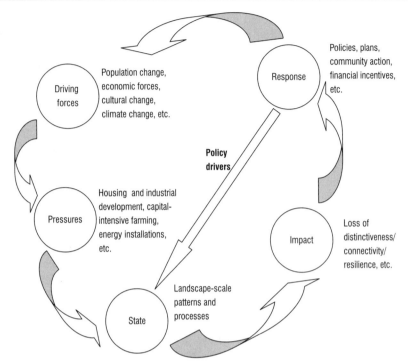

Figure 3.1 An illustrative DPSIR model for the cultural landscape

This framework is an extension of the pressure–state–response model developed by the Organisation of Economic Co-operation and Development (1993) and has been widely adopted (e.g. European Environment Agency, 1995) as a way of organizing evidence and analysis in pursuit of environmental interventions. Through the use of the DPSIR modelling framework, it is possible to identify connections between its different elements and gauge the effectiveness of responses put into place (Schneeberger et al., 2007). Driving forces, such as population and economic growth, urbanization and agricultural intensification, result in emissions of pollutants and other pressures that affect the state of the environment and, in turn, may impact on human health or ecosystems. Responses may address the driving forces themselves as well as seek to reduce their direct pressures or indirect effects on the state of the environment and human health. Responses, such as policies and plans, can themselves become significant drivers: for example agricultural policy during the twentieth century successfully promoted widespread intensification and increased productivity of land use. Overall, the key message is that the dynamic landscape is constantly subject to 'change drivers' (Figure 3.1).

A useful indication of the nature of future drivers of change was provided by a horizon-scanning study commissioned by Natural England (2009d), looking fifty years into the future from 2010, and this identified thirteen key 'influencers' on the future landscape (Box 3.1). As noted above, planning and

Box 3.1 Potential key drivers of landscape change in the twenty-first century (based on Natural England, 2009d; Creedy et al., 2009)

- Climate change – a driver with both physical and social impacts. Whilst direct physical changes are relatively well predicted, there is far more uncertainty about the indirect changes associated with the ways in which people will respond. Further, whilst the likely broad trends are quite well understood, there are many uncertainties surrounding the future rate, type and eventual magnitude of change.
- Converging new technologies – resulting in massive changes in relation to new products and services, as well as in reshaping societal relationships. Nanotechnologies and bioengineering will bring about extensive change in manufacturing and food production, blurring the line between life and the inorganic world, modifying plants, animals and micro-organisms and, ultimately, designing entirely novel forms of life. Information technology will spread from silicon into bio- and nano-carriers, and become pervasive.
- Demographics – the human race is increasing in numbers and is rapidly migrating to urban centres. The global population, currently around 7 billion, is expected to peak at around 10 billion during this century. Natural resources and ecosystem services will come under increasing pressure. Most growth will come from extended lifespan so that, by 2060, the population everywhere will be much older than it is now.
- Energy – historically, this has been a major driver of landscape change. The world is approaching peak global oil and gas production, and demand is increasing rapidly, especially from the emerging economies. Even with the development of renewable alternatives, it is likely that the scarcity and cost of energy will change many of our land uses and activities. By 2060 global energy supply is likely to be far more diverse and the energy mix will be made up of both existing low carbon technologies and new technologies.
- Food security – perhaps the most fundamental driver of all. Even though the world now appears to be feeding itself quite well, this is at least partly because of heavy mineral and energy subsidies, and their pollution effects, that may not be sustainable in the long term. As population and wealth increase, global demand for food is growing faster than global supply. The situation is complicated because the effects of short-term supply–demand cycles and weather impacts on crop yields is superimposed on top of long-term changes.
- World economic power shifts – especially as emerging economies such as the BRIC countries – Brazil, Russia, India and China – gain dominance. With huge populations and growing gross domestic product (GDP), their political, social and ethical influence will rise.
- Governance – the world is anticipated to become an increasingly dangerous place, so future governance may well be dominated by concerns to increase resilience and reduce risk.
- Health and well-being – despite increased longevity, health and well-being, there will be particular problems associated with preventable lifestyle diseases (mainly associated with unhealthy lifestyles and diets). Infectious diseases in humans, animals and plants will increase, amplified by the effects of climate change.
- Marine environments – deterioration of seas, due to acidification, pollution and over-fishing may lead to disastrous collapses in fish populations. Plastics and plastic particles are a growing problem in the oceans, whilst absorbed carbon

Continued ...

Box 3.1 continued

dioxide exhausts oceans' ability to buffer the excess amount in the atmosphere, accelerating acidification.

- Mobility – transport will continue to increase and will precipitate many landscape changes, but it is possible that most travel worldwide will be for leisure, and virtuality will be used for business contacts. Migration will also increase as globalization encourages labour mobility, and populations shift following war, environmental degradation or climate change.

- Money, wealth, economy – there may well be new models of economic activity, such as the possibility of a different model of manufacturing based on localized production, or variations from the current free-market Western paradigm.

- Resources – economic growth and the associated growth in consumption among emerging economies is resulting in a worldwide rush for resources, and there are particular concerns over water shortages and food security. However, there may be a growing commitment to ensuring that resources are used efficiently, and to improved reuse and recycling technologies.

- Values – what we are prepared to accept or positively want to see helps to shape our landscape. Our values will be influenced by the pervasive, immersive information and media technologies based on open source architecture. Global levels of education will continue to rise. Possibly, a scientific worldview will emerge that is underpinned by paradigms of chaos and complexity. Better connectivity through IT may promote bottom-up civic engagement.

policy have become significant drivers in their own right, and the synthesis in Table 3.1 points to the specific responses by public agencies to external pressures on the landscape.

Sometimes, change may be relatively accepted or unnoticed, and at other times vehemently contested. Opposition to change may be for strong ethical or scientific reasons, but it may also be related to personal values and preferences. For example, visually intrusive wind turbines might be accepted by some because they appear graceful and majestic, convey explicit evidence of a more sustainable society, and possibly bring financial benefits to the local community. Others may see them as an eyesore, not only because of visual aesthetics, but also because they cognitively associate wind power with unproven, inefficient technology (Selman, 2010a).

It appears that various factors influence people's response to landscape change (Natural England, 2009a). First is the degree to which change is isolated and widespread or subtle and striking. As might be anticipated, changes that are striking and/or extensive tend to be most easily noticed. However, the incremental effect of smaller change can become significant. Second is the extent to which people are affected by the change. People will be more inclined to be content or concerned depending on the effect of any change on them or people they know. However, some less immediate changes may have indirect, diffuse or delayed effects that result in uncertainty and apprehension. Third is the degree of influence that people feel they have

Table 3.1 Desirable drivers of landscape change and key delivery mechanisms for their attainment (based on Landscape Character Network, 2009)

	Drivers	*Deliverers (examples)*	*Interactions with landscape*
Economic	• economic growth and employment • regeneration • developing sustainable communities	• central government and its agencies • utility companies and infrastructure providers • development companies • tourism partnerships	• importance of landscape to recreation and tourism • landscape helps create 'place' – attractive to businesses, residents and inward investment • sustainable development needs to be based on local environmental limits and capacities
Social	• community cohesion and volunteering • social learning • health and quality of life • place-making	• central government and its agencies • local authorities and partnerships (e.g. health authorities) • education and transport sectors	• character-based landscape planning and recreation/access • interpretation and education • place-based green infrastructure • landscape objectives based on understanding of societal values
Environmental	• climate change mitigation and adaptation • natural resource protection • conservation and enhancement of biodiversity • cultural heritage and ecosystem services	• central government and its agencies • local and national park authorities • NGOs • landowners, developers and utility companies	• integrated landscape and green infrastructure planning as context for climate change adaptation, biodiversity • landscape protection, management and planning for multiple benefits

over the change. Is change, for example, being driven by powerful outside investors or by locally based social entrepreneurs? In addition to landscape change, there will also be a co-evolutionary change in people's attitudes. Some landscape changes may initially meet widespread resistance but slowly gain social approval; others may initially be scarcely noticed but later may be opposed. Both the actual landscape changes and the changing human response to the changes are difficult to anticipate.

Vulnerability and resilience in landscapes

One of the key arguments surrounding the issue of landscape connectivity is the effect of change on resilience. Broadly speaking, it can be assumed that a fragmented and degraded landscape will lose its resilience to future stresses, but that reinstating functional connectivity will tend to improve its adaptive capacity. A great deal of policy and scientific interest has recently centred on the notion of resilience (Walker and Salt, 2006). In some theories of resilience, the focus of attention is on the adaptive potential of social–ecological systems. As noted previously, we use 'social' as a catch-all term for human dimensions such as culture, society, economy and learning, whilst 'ecology' is used in an equally broad way to include all biological and physical environmental systems. It can be argued that social–ecological systems have many similarities to cultural landscapes as landscape is the dynamic arena in which society and ecology gel (Box 3.2).

The social–ecological system concept is particularly useful in relation to ecosystem dynamics, where natural and human influences can cause ecosystems to 'tip' into a different state. 'Tipping points' can result in social–ecological systems shifting to a less desirable state in human and ecological terms, and decision makers may therefore seek to make the system more resilient and adaptive, giving 'space' to innate checks and balances in the system that will reduce the likelihood of a catastrophic shift. (Note that entirely natural processes can tip systems into a state that appears disastrous for biodiversity, although, over time, evolutionary processes will lead to creative recovery. The situation considered in this chapter is where significant damage has been inflicted on biodiversity by processes that include a non-benign human influence.) Human responses to resilience promotion involve two main changes of approach: first, planners and managers move away from trying to stop change and instead try to facilitate conditions in which systems are able to adapt to short-term shocks and long-term progressive change; second, land users and conservation managers are seen as integral parts of the system rather than as external controllers of it.

Landscape is the milieu wherein human and ecological systems are integrated, and these systems support a range of functions. In their natural state these systems tend to be inherently regenerative when viewed over sufficiently long timescales. However, in social–ecological systems, especially

Box 3.2 Principal areas of similarity between social–ecological systems and cultural landscapes (based on Selman, 2012)

Social–ecological systems and cultural landscapes:

- comprise a combination of social (governmental, economic, human, built) and ecological (biotic, physical) subsystems;
- have governance and management mechanisms that are internal, rather than external, to the system;
- require the conservation of slow change variables if they are to evolve through different adaptive cycles in ways that sustain human well-being and continue to furnish information about wise use;
- evolve through adaptive cycles in ways that retain critical forms and functions, even though their associated production and consumption activities change;
- may respond to internal and external change drivers by shifting into alternative stable states over time in relatively unpredictable ways;
- may, under conditions of excessive exploitation, transform into less desirable states that may prove highly resistant to change;
- constantly intersect with various temporal and spatial scales, via processes of upscaling/downscaling (e.g. local biodiversity responses to global climatic changes) and cross-scaling (e.g. connections to adjacent agricultural regimes);
- may spontaneously engender virtuous cycles within social and ecological subsystems, which lead to synergy between sustainable entrepreneurship, food security, social capital and psychological well-being;
- are defined by common internal elements, such as spatial system properties (size, boundaries), spatial variations in ecosystem succession, and subsystems and their interactions;
- are sensitive to common external elements, such as spatial connectivities, cross-boundary energy and nutrient subsidies, and spatially driven feedbacks;
- possess a certain level of resilience that depends on the number and nature of components and interactions, the ability of the system to undergo change while maintaining identity and memory, and an inherent potential for adaptation and learning;
- display emergent qualities deriving from processes operating at discontinuities and thresholds associated with adaptive cycles operating at discrete scales.

where human use has lacked wisdom and sensitivity, processes can quickly become degenerate. It might be argued that excessively simplified social–ecological systems are characterized by the dominant human exploitation of a narrow range of functions, reducing the overall level of landscape/ecosystem services. In such simplified systems, interconnections are disrupted. This affects both the physical links between natural systems and the associative links between people and place. It has been contended that multifunctional landscapes are more resilient to change, and can adapt to future shocks not least because they invoke 'intelligent care' from human communities, and this possibility will be discussed further in due course. Where landscapes become less resilient, they may lose some of their values, though this may not readily be apparent to society, mainly because loss tends to occur in services that have no immediate market price. Indeed, many mono-functional landscapes appear to have very high values because, with sufficient artificial subsidies of energy and materials, they continue to yield high outputs of desired goods and services. However, unsustainable use will tend to reduce even economic values in the long term.

Another key focus of policy interest has been the notion of sustainability. This is now such a dominant theme that it can be taken as one of the main 'narratives' around which modern society organizes itself. Sustainability still remains an elusive and contested concept and, given the complexity of what we mean by landscape, the notion of landscape sustainability becomes almost ineffable. Pragmatically, though, we can see landscape sustainability in terms of:

- Environmental sustainability – a biodiverse landscape capable of self-regulation, within manageable and acceptable levels of risk and hazard.
- Social sustainability – where there is a 'just' allocation of landscape quality and risk, and where there are abundant levels of memory, attachment and 'good' social capital.
- Economic sustainability – where economic practices incidentally 'pay' for landscape, and the landscape helps to sustain jobs (e.g. through green tourism), supports embedded economic practices, and yields wholesome, traceable food.
- Aesthetic sustainability – where the visual and ecological aesthetic coincide, so that ecological resilience is 'sensed' through the appearance of the landscape.
- Policy sustainability – where modes of governance are transparent and inclusive, and deliver value for money within acceptable levels of bureaucracy and taxpayer subvention (Selman, 2008).

Sustaining the multifunctionality of cultural landscapes is thus a balance between nurturing inherited resources and adapting to dynamic drivers. Disconnected from the evidence around us and from other wisdoms than our own, we can too easily fail to exercise intelligent care of the landscape. Some landscapes have already seriously degenerated and require concerted intervention if they are to supply ecosystem services of acceptable value to nature and society.

A key argument for landscape reconnection is that a landscape in which functionality is widely restored is likely to be more resilient, and less vulnerable to future shocks. In practice, it will have more possibilities to adjust to perturbation and to regain a dynamic equilibrium. As will be noted shortly, there is a difference between 'resilience' as a general term and the more formal concept of 'resilience theory'.

This book assumes that connectedness in landscape systems is broadly desirable. In the resilience literature, however, over-connection in social–

ecological systems is seen as potentially leading to dissipative behaviour in which systems become 'brittle' and tend to 'revolt'. This is referring to a different notion of connection, although the terminology can be confusing. For example, if a small and isolated nature reserve with vulnerable species is highly dependent on numerous specific relationships being maintained – such as those linking feeding requirements at specific stages of an insect's lifecycle – then one small change, such as slightly earlier or later seasons due to climate change, may lead to major alterations in ecosystem patterns and processes. Similarly, changed management interventions in a highly modified ecosystem, such as intensification or de-intensification of livestock grazing, can have many consequences because of the numerous brittle links between different plants and animals, as well as soil and hydrological impacts. Perhaps a further analogy can be made with social capital. Communities that have strong bonding and bridging capital are likely to be resilient to crisis, pulling together in times of adversity and cooperating entrepreneurially in times of opportunity. By contrast, political and economic situations that are highly dependent on a filigree of negotiated agreements and contractual relationships may be highly vulnerable to loss of trust or unexpected impacts. The crisis in Western financial systems that commenced in 2008 is often seen as a case of brittleness caused by over-connection, where success or failure in national economies and financial institutions was related to fragile contingencies between international debt liabilities. It is therefore plausible that reciprocity that is broadly and deeply seated will promote adaptability and the emergence of stable new forms, but that reliance on numerous expedient 'fixes' may ultimately lead to system failure.

Despite the fact that resilience – and its counterpoint, vulnerability – has become such a central concept across numerous policy areas, there is no commonly used definition in an environmental context. The Department for Environment, Food and Rural Affairs (2010) referred to resilience of the environment to withstand change while still providing the 'ecosystem services' that people enjoy. This statement was based on Demos's interpretation of resilience as the capacity of an individual, community or system to adapt in order to sustain an acceptable level of function, structure and identity (Edwards, 2009). Resilience implies the ability of the system to bounce back, or return to some quasi-stable state.

Woodroffe (2007), considering the resilience of the coastal system, suggested that 'vulnerability' is the degree to which a coast is likely to be adversely affected by, or its incapability to withstand the consequences of, impact. The impact may be from a natural event such as a storm or flood, or from human actions and events. At the coast, the principal climate change driver is likely to be a growing vulnerability to sea level rise, although there are also various other related impacts. Vulnerability is multidimensional, covering both the physical and ecological response of the coast, as well as economic, institutional and sociocultural dimensions. The coast can be viewed as an interconnected natural and socio-economic system, possessing both susceptibility and sensitivity. Susceptibility describes the system's innate potential to be affected, whereas sensitivity refers to its responsiveness, and thus the likelihood of changing or failing. Its natural ability to respond can be viewed in terms of the resistance of the coast, which includes the mechanical strength of materials, structural and morphological resistance, and its ability to filter the sea's energy. However, the overall resilience of a coast, defined as its ability to resist change in functions or processes, relates both to natural susceptibility and sensitivity, and to a range of social, cultural and institutional inputs to the coastal management process (McFadden, 2010).

In relation to biodiversity, resilience has been referred to as the ability of a set of mutually reinforcing structures and processes to persist, rather than shift and become organized around another set of processes and structures. The resilience of a specific ecological organization is measured by the amount of change that a system can experience before it is forced to reorganize (The Wildlife Trusts, 2007). It has been suggested that we can lose resilience if our environment, society and economy are close to 'tipping points'. For example, the London Climate Change Project (2009) noted how the effects of climate change might exacerbate other threats impacting on biodiversity. In other words, the stress of climate change could push the system beyond its tipping point because the system's resilience had been eroded by other factors. Thus, resilience of ecosystems and species was being undermined by trends such as:

- abandonment of management, leading to scrub encroachment (e.g. semi-natural grassland habitats);
- nutrient enrichment and pollution (e.g. decline in otter populations nationally is strongly linked to pollution by polychlorinated biphenyls and organochlorine pesticides);
- over-abstraction of water (e.g. impacts on streams fed by chalk aquifers);
- aerial pollutants (e.g. the inner urban lichen flora is often impoverished as a result of susceptibility to aerial pollution);
- existing fragmentation of habitat, resulting in the diminution of populations to levels that are now too small and isolated to be viable in the long term;
- growing population, bringing with it competition for natural resources that are shared by wildlife such as water and soils, and pressure from visitors that disturbs sensitive species.

The Lawton Review (Lawton et al., 2010) defined a 'coherent' ecological network as one that has all the elements necessary to achieve its overall objectives; the components are chosen to be complementary and mutually reinforcing so that the value of the whole network is greater than the sum

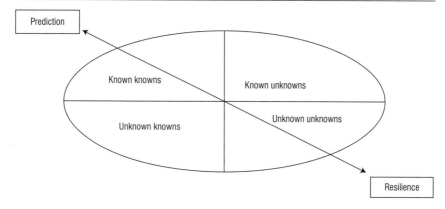

Figure 3.2 Combinations of knowable and unknowable circumstances in future situations (based on ideas widely attributed to Rumsfeld)

of its parts. It defined a 'resilient' ecological network as one that is capable of absorbing, resisting or recovering from disturbances and damage caused by natural perturbations and human activities (including climate change) while continuing to meet its overall objectives of supporting biodiversity and providing ecosystem services. The overall message of the Lawton Review was to 'make space' for nature so that it was less hemmed in and disrupted by ecologically hostile land uses, and so that new connections, migrations and communities might flourish.

Resilience theory, it could be argued, aims to promote the management of social–ecological systems in ways that reduce the risk of their 'tipping' into a less desirable state from which it is difficult to recover. One key idea appears to be that economic and political systems (and their associated natural resource management systems) conventionally rely on predictive modelling based on past trends to predict future situations, and then aim to control change in accordance with preferred outcomes. By contrast, resilience theory suggests that hyper-complex systems will be impossible to predict, or to control from the 'outside', and so their survival will depend on promoting resilience and innate capacity to recover from future, and sometimes unforeseeable, shocks.

This dilemma can be related to former US Defense Secretary Donald Rumsfeld's well known taxonomy of known and unknown external circumstances (Figure 3.2). Natural resource planning and management has tended to assume a situation of 'known knowns' – we know past trends, and so we know how to construct models that predict the future so we can apply well tested engineering solutions to manage foreseeable problems and opportunities. Sometimes information is an 'unknown known' – it is known in some quarters, but is not necessarily known to some people who need the information, such as military satellite information on land use trends that would be valuable to civil society. Sometimes we are well aware that a factor will raise challenges for human society even though we do not know precisely how it will manifest itself – it will be a 'known unknown' like the consequences of potentially increased coastal risk to storm surges. However, there are some significant future shocks that we cannot prepare for because we do not even know what they will be. Broadly speaking, over the past generation we have moved from a mindset of planning and managing 'known knowns' to one of preparing for 'unknown unknowns'. The latter can only be addressed by building up general social–ecological resilience and adaptive capacity, rather than relying on specific predict-and-control measures. Hence, resilience theory is leading us towards goals of reinforcing and reinstating landscape functions and services, and of promoting social and institutional learning.

Building social resilience

Social resilience can be accumulated in various ways, for instance through building capacity and through preparing for emergencies (Berkes and Folke, 1998). Central to social resilience is the process of social learning, accompanied by institutional learning; in an environmental context these are sometimes referred to as sustainability learning. Jiggins et al. (2007) identify social resilience as a way of adapting in the face of surprise, which is necessary because some drivers, such as climate change and flooding, have an irreducible level of uncertainty. They specifically refer to the situation in The Netherlands, where the historical policy imperative has been to prevent flooding, but where there is now a growing recognition that water needs to be 'given space' in order to regain a new equilibrium. This clearly causes major challenges in a crowded country where space is already occupied by multiple other users and functions. The emerging policy situation, however, recognizes that water management can no longer just be left to experts and specialists, or plans based solely on past experience. Thus, new institutional arrangements need to evolve. The authors argue that where the future policy direction is unclear, and new approaches and assumptions have to be explored, 'double loop learning' becomes necessary. This is characterized by questions that probe the underlying assumptions embedded in cognitive frames and behaviour, so that new values and new visions of the future are explored and formulated, possibly leading to radical changes in institutional behaviour.

Jiggins et al. (2007) found that social resilience requires styles of leadership that emphasize values rather than entirely rational goals, and which motivate organizational change and create conditions for exploration of new challenges and actions. Rather than work within a hierarchical structure, social and institutional learning appears to require 'loosely coupled' networks that reach out to include new actors who encounter each other in new social spaces. Organizational renewal begins to emerge from those interactions that, over time, re-stabilize as a new wisdom. This requires an emphasis on knowledge development that, rather than technology or policy, is posited as the primary driver of transformational change. It challenges previously stabilized knowledge in which experts assume that stakeholders have a 'knowledge deficit' that needs to be remedied by having the preferred solution explained to them. Instead it requires knowledge to be exchanged between social spaces in different sectors, professions and disciplines so that knowledge management gives way to knowledge development. None of this comes easily to scientists and policy makers steeped in conventional information production and delivery – nor should it, or else rigorous standards of practice may be compromised. However, over time, new modes of knowledge development will encourage essential social and institutional adaptation.

Kabat et al. (2006) also drew upon the Dutch 'Living with Water' programme as an illustration of social and institutional learning, in particular referring to its central concept of 'climate proofing'. This includes the use of conventional grey infrastructure to reduce risks to a quantified level, accepted by the society or economy. This risk is mitigated by social capacity including insurance schemes and evacuation plans. In view of the increasing use of storm surge barriers to control floods, the 'Living with Water' strategy shifts towards accommodating extreme climate events rather than fighting them with heavy infrastructure, and accommodating and carefully managing periodic flooding in specific designated areas (Figure 3.3). Resilience is also being built in relation to other climate-related changes, such as the increased frequency of summer droughts. For instance, farmers are being supported to diversify their activities and move away from conventional productivist agriculture. More radically still, urban and industrial activities, including infrastructure, could progressively be moved from below sea level to higher and drier ground, or could even be created in a 'hydrometropole' – a major conurbation partly floating on and surrounded by water, where people have learned how to live with and make a living from water.

Petts (2006), reporting on the experience of an urban flood management project in an English city, referred to the importance of 'framing' issues in a collaborative way. Where stakeholders were constructively involved, social learning tended to occur through a balancing act between public concerns and expert technical discourses. In this case study, the multidisciplinary expert team — ecologists, hydrologists, landscape designers, architects, land use planners, project managers, pollution control officers and flood control planners — were challenged at the outset to recognize the relative value of different types of knowledge, including those emanating from the local community. The culture of expertise witnessed at the beginning of the process was the typical 'deficit' model, in effect, based on the 'myth of the best argument' (Pellizzoni, 2001): at this stage, most of the practitioners had not previously taken part in a public process where they needed to prioritize

Figure 3.3 A recently established flood meadow in Gelderland, The Netherlands, managed for biodiversity and periodic floodwater storage

skills of observation, listening, presentation, discussion and debating. Thus, the exercise sought to embrace a diversity of arguments and perspectives by capitalizing on the potential of the deliberative process, and relied on creating and managing the right conditions to support learning. This entailed exploring the ways in which experts frame the explanation of and solutions to a situation, whilst at the same time ensuring that local knowledge and public issues and priorities are tensioned against what is practically achievable. The author argued that social learning and capacity building were most likely to occur when there is: quality time for expert–lay interaction; facilitated co-construction of the problem and definition of community priorities as well as technical principles; and a continuous effort to promote agreement on the actions needed, combined with a shared recognition of the practical constraints.

Social resilience may also be related to the rich social capital that can be invested in places that possess reserves of identity, attachment, pride, care and involvement (Czerniak, 2007). As noted previously, urban designers have suggested that a 'sense of place' can be closely linked to a locality's resilience and sustainability. Key ideas that emerge from policy and research are that: places are better if communities are actively engaged in shaping them; distinctive places can support strong but not exclusive identities; strong and confident communities are, through their bridging capital, welcoming to new people; culture, history, heritage and the historic environment can enable people to learn about their area; and the more actively people are involved in shaping local culture and heritage the stronger their sense of local identity is likely to be.

Resilience theory

Resilience theory goes beyond the popular conception of resilience. Although the theory remains quite controversial in some quarters, it has introduced concepts and vocabulary that have gained widespread application. Redman and Kinzig (2003) identify the concern of resilience theory as lying with 'adaptive systems', in other words, complex social–ecological systems that adapt in often unpredictable ways to changes that are caused by natural and human drivers. Some changes will be damped by feedback effects and the system will tend to return more or less to its previous state. Occasionally changes will trigger effects that are amplified by feedback, and a transformative change will occur, so that the system may move to another state. Thus, resilience theory seeks to understand the source and role of change in adaptive systems, particularly those kinds of change that are transforming (Holling and Gunderson, 2002). It seeks to do this by studying dynamic cycles that are linked across spatial and temporal scales. There is also evidence that the elusive landscape property of 'emergence' tends to occur at the boundaries of these spatial and temporal scales (Garmestani et al., 2009). Cumming (2011) has referred to the notion of 'spatial resilience', and this provides a direct way of linking social–ecological resilience to cultural landscapes.

At the core of resilience theory is the adaptive cycle, in which growth and conservation of resources is followed by release and reorganization of resources. This may result in changes that are frequently not dissimilar to 'succession' in classic ecosystem theory; however, critically, adaptive cycles allow for greater surprise and unpredictability in the emergence of new social–ecological systems rather than the deterministic model of succession towards a climatic climax ecological system. Individual adaptive cycles are nested in a hierarchy across time and space. These nested hierarchies may have a stabilizing effect due to the fact that they provide 'memory' of historically and spatially linked cycles that allow recovery and re-stabilization after change occurs. Memory may include both human memory of previous events and responses, and the physical and biological repository of processes and materials that can anchor a system in deeper, more stable states. However, sometimes dynamics across scales become brittle due to natural processes of progression from one habitat type to another or to disruptive human intervention. Where this is the case, small-scale transformations may revolt rather than return to their former state, and explode into larger-scale crises. Taken together, the multiple adaptive cycles and the processes that determine their system states are referred to as 'panarchy' (Holling and Gunderson, 2002).

Resilience is the ability to absorb disturbances, to be changed and then to reorganize and still have the same identity (retain the same basic structure and ways of functioning). It includes the ability to learn, or gain memory, from the disturbance. A resilient system is forgiving of external shocks. As resilience declines, the magnitude of a shock from which the system can recover gets smaller and smaller. Conventional policy goals – such as growth and efficiency – can drive systems into fragile rigidities, exposing them to turbulent transformation; by contrast, learning, recovery and flexibility can lead to novelty and new worlds of opportunity. The aims of resilience management and governance are either to keep the system within a particular configuration of states or 'regimes' that will continue to deliver desired ecosystem goods and services (preventing the system from moving into an undesirable regime from which it is either difficult or impossible to recover), or to move from a less desirable to a more desirable regime. Various concepts have been identified that help these aims to be pursued in resilience-based policy and management (Box 3.3).

The underlying assumptions of resilience theory are highly complex, but their essence can be summarized in terms of three key features. First, change in ecological systems is neither continuous and gradual nor always chaotic. Rather, it is episodic, with periods of slow accumulation of 'natural capital' punctuated by sudden releases and reorganizations of those legacies. This episodic behaviour is caused by interactions between fast variables (e.g. wildfires) and slow variables (e.g. soil development). Second, spatial and temporal attributes mean that system behaviour differs at different scales and in response to very local and detailed differences, so it is not possible to predict the behaviour of a system simply by scaling up or down from smaller or larger ones. Patterns and processes are patchy and discontinuous at all scales. Third, resilience theory contrasts with the 'classical' model of ecosystems, which assumes a predictable progression through various stages (seres) to a climatic climax biotope, which is then maintained by homeostatic controls as a delicately balanced dynamic equilibrium. More recent ecological theory suggests that there is not a single equilibrium towards which an ecosystem will mature; rather, there may be multiple equilibria that can result in different but equally stable ecosystem states. Scheffer et al. (2001) note that, even in apparently stable landscapes, external conditions – such as climate, nutrient inputs, toxic chemicals, groundwater depletion, habitat fragmentation, harvesting or biodiversity loss – often change gradually over time. In practice, the state of some ecosystems may respond in a smooth, continuous way to such trends, whereas others may hardly appear to change at all but then

---

Box 3.3 Key concepts relating to the resilience of social–ecological systems

- Non-linearity – because of non-linear dynamics many systems can exist in 'alternative stable states' with distinctive regimes and thresholds. The state of a system is defined by the amounts of variables that constitute the system (e.g. grass, shrubs, livestock); the state space is the three-dimensional space of all possible combinations of the amounts of these variables; and the dynamics of the system are reflected as its movement through this space. The system thus keeps basically the same structure and function, albeit in different configurations/regimes.

- System states are referred to as 'basins of attraction' (spaces within which a system will remain, allowing for considerable turbulence, but tending to recover and re-stabilize within this same broad 'basin'). Considerable disturbance is needed for a regime to cross the threshold that separates one basin from another but, once crossed, the system will re-stabilize in this different basin. Crossing the threshold backwards to return to the original basin is very difficult. Thus, alternate regimes are separated by thresholds that are marked by key variables that determine the broad system state. The feedback effect of these variables is the cause of change in function and therefore structure.

- Adaptive cycles – social–ecological systems, like all systems, are never static, and tend to move through recurring phases (the adaptive cycle). In its simplest form, this has a double loop – a more-or-less predictable and relatively long 'foreloop' (the growth and conservation phase) and a rapid, chaotic 'backloop' (the release and reorganization phase).

- Multiple scales and cross-scale effects (panarchy) – no system can be understood or managed by focusing on it at a single scale. All social–ecological systems exist and function at multiple scales of space, time and social organization (panarchy), and the interactions across scales are fundamentally important in determining the dynamics of the system at any particular focal scale.

- Adaptability and transformability – adaptability is the capacity of a social–ecological system to manage resilience in relation to alternative regimes. For this, we need to be able to determine the trajectory of the system state (its position within its current basin of attraction) and the ability to alter the shape of the basins (move the position of the thresholds or change the system's resistance to perturbation). If the social–ecological system is already in an undesirable regime, one option is to transform it into a different kind of system, for example through sensitive large-scale reclamation or pursuing fundamentally different modes of economic activity.

- General versus specified resilience – specified resilience is the resilience of a part of a system to a particular event, but in complex systems with uncertain futures it is necessary to build up a more general resilience.

Source: Adapted from Resilience Alliance,
http://www.resalliance.org/index.php/key_concepts.

---

suddenly respond dramatically when conditions approach a certain critical level. Both smooth and sudden changes can result in a social–ecological system passing a critical threshold into a different system state.

Thus, resilience theorists dispute the idea of an inexorable natural progression towards a unique and stable climax. They argue that, for certain environmental conditions, the ecosystem may have two or more alternative stable states, separated by an unstable equilibrium that marks the border between the 'basins of attraction' of these states. The existence of a lag, or inertia, between alternative stable states separated by a regime shift, is referred to as hysteresis. Thus, inertia in a system may both delay a regime shift even though the tipping point has passed, so that a crisis may not be manifest until it is too late, and it will also result in great effort being needed to reverse a regime shift to a system state that occurred well before the tipping point. Land use policies and land management methods can lead to brittleness or over-connection, ultimately leading to system 'revolt', especially where they apply fixed rules for achieving constant yields from an ecosystem, independent of the complex sensitivities of a particular location. Such land use practices will engineer the flexibility out of adaptive cycles, leading to systems that increasingly lose resilience and can thus suddenly break down in the face of disturbances that previously could be absorbed.

Because ecosystems are moving targets, planning and management have to be flexible and work at scales that are compatible with the scales of critical ecosystem and social functions. A central message of resilience theory is that individuals, their institutions, and society at large need to develop ways of learning from past experiences, as well as learning to live with some natural hazards and uncertainties. An interesting perspective on this has been provided by Redman and Kinzig (2003), who explained very long-term social change in terms of resilience theory. Drawing upon rich archaeological evidence (specifically, case studies of Mesopotamia and the desert areas of south-western USA), they were able to study complete cycles of society–environment relationships. They concluded that the key to enhancing resilience lay in improving our ability to understand 'early warning' signals of undesirable state change, and our capacity to adapt. This would require fuller knowledge of the critical scales at which signals emerge and the development of more responsive institutions.

Bolliger et al. (2003) refer to the self-organization that occurs over the evolution of a landscape where system properties emerge spontaneously, driven internally by variations of the system itself. This would help to explain why many of the most desired qualities of cultural landscapes, such as distinctive character and multifunctionality, are emergent properties. Self-organization occurs simultaneously across different orders of magnitude. Although the concept of 'landscape scale' remains central, there is no single landscape scale, but a panarchy of interactions across multiple scales. Consequently, society–nature needs sufficient space, place and time for processes to operate in a sustainable and resilient way throughout a multifunctional landscape in order to sustain a requisite diversity of ecosystem services.

The presence of alternative stable states has profound implications for the way in which an ecosystem will respond to change. When a social–ecological

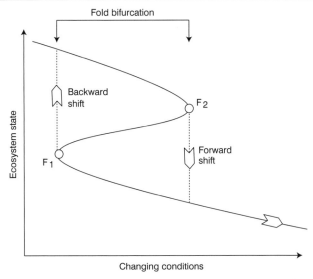

Figure 3.4 Transformative change in a social–ecological system (based on Scheffer et al., 2001)

system is in a state on the upper branch of the folded curve, it cannot pass to the lower branch smoothly (Figure 3.4). Instead, when conditions change sufficiently to pass the threshold, referred to as a saddle-node or fold bifurcation, a catastrophic transition to the lower branch occurs (i.e. transformative change). Although this lower branch may be equally stable and resistant to change, it is also likely to possess a lower level of complexity. Since complex systems are normally more supportive of a variety of life and better able to adapt to processes of change, the lower branch may be deemed to be less resilient. It is quite common for little change to be observed in a system state before this switch occurs. Due to the effects of hysteresis, catastrophic shifts typically occur quite unannounced, and give off few early-warning signals. Another important feature is that in order to move a system back to the upper branch, it is not sufficient simply to restore environmental conditions to those that prevailed before the collapse. Instead, one needs to go back further, beyond the first switch point. If the original system state was considered preferable, then recovering this will require massive effort, and may indeed prove impossible. In nature, changes occur in system states due to stochastic events such as severe weather conditions. If a system type has only one basin of attraction, it will settle back to essentially the same state after these disturbances. However, if there are alternative stable states, a sufficiently severe perturbation of the ecosystem state may bring the system into the basin of attraction of another state. Resilience theorists have related stability to the size of the basin of attraction around a state, which corresponds to the maximum perturbation that can be taken without causing a shift to an alternative stable state.

Scheffer et al. (2001) note that in systems with multiple stable states, gradually changing conditions may have little effect on the state of the ecosystem, although they may reduce the size of the attraction basin. This causes a loss of resilience, making the system more fragile and more prone to being tipped into a contrasting state by stochastic events. In terms of biodiversity conservation management, the key issue is that stability domains typically depend on slowly changing variables such as land use, nutrient stocks, soil properties and the biomass of long-lived organisms. These factors may be predicted, monitored and modified. By contrast, stochastic events that trigger state shifts are usually difficult to predict or control. Traditional conservation management has often tried to focus its efforts on avoiding or fixing the results of stochastic changes such as harsh winters and wildfires. However, resilience theory suggests that long-term success is more likely to be based on building the underlying resilience of desired ecosystem states, in other words ensuring the fundamental health and functionality of slowly changing variables, thereby maintaining the size of the attraction basin. Whilst homeostatic forces exist within social–ecological systems, so do destabilizing forces such as landslips and microclimate changes. Destabilizing forces are important in maintaining diversity, flexibility and opportunity, whilst homeostatic forces help to maintain productivity, fixed capital and social memory. This broad approach can be extended from managing natural ecosystems for biodiversity conservation, to the wider challenge of planning and managing complex social–ecological systems for human survival and well-being.

Broadly, the significance of resilience theory for the maintenance of adaptive capacity in cultural landscapes can be distilled into three principles (Walker et al., 2002). First, resilience theory concerns the amount of change a system can undergo – the amount of stress it can sustain – and still retain broadly its same functionality and structure, and remain in the same configuration or domain/basin of attraction. Second, a system is characterized by the degree to which it is capable of self-organization. When managers or policy makers control certain variables in a system, they cause responses that would not be there without their intervention; the more 'self-organizing' the system, the fewer feedbacks need to be introduced by managers. Third is the degree to which the system expresses capacity for learning and adaptation. Overall, resilience is the potential of a system to remain in a particular configuration and to maintain its feedbacks and functions despite disturbances, and it involves the ability of the system to reorganize following change. Adaptive capacity is an aspect of resilience that reflects learning, flexibility, experimentation and novel solutions. It entails the development of generalized responses to broad classes of challenges.

Regenerative social–ecological systems – building resilience

Resilience theory suggests that policy and management for cultural landscapes should aim to make them more generally resilient to a range of disturbances, including unexpected conditions. This entails building adaptive capacity in the system. Like social capital, resilience may not always be desirable: system configurations that decrease social welfare, such as polluted water supplies or dictatorships display many of the characteristics of a resilient system, in a very stable basin of attraction. As with social capital, resilience may be 'good' or 'bad'. Since some undesired social–ecological configurations may be both resistant and resilient, we need a socially endorsed touchstone to judge whether a system is showing the right kind of resilience. It has been proposed, therefore, that measures to promote resilience should be tested in relation to their sustainability, including principles of social justice (Selman, 2012). Whilst sustainability is a contested concept, nonetheless it has been widely debated and endorsed by society and government, and may reasonably be taken as a broad social consensus. In turn, decisions about landscape should be democratized as far as possible, and in subsequent sections we consider how this might be achieved via landscape quality objectives, supported by community participation and social learning opportunities.

As we have seen, approaches to natural resource management have conventionally aimed to predict likely effects of management and trends in external drivers such as climate (Walker et al., 2004). They also tend to assume that the manager is outside the system being managed. Such approaches have generally yielded positive responses in relation to short-term planning horizons. However, when the aim is to pursue long-term sustainability, resilience theorists have suggested that it is inappropriate to treat the environment as a separate entity, such as a natural or agricultural ecosystem. Over long timescales, uncertainties are large and it may be difficult to reduce them as fast as the system changes. Building resilience involves maintaining the functionality of a system when it is perturbed, or maintaining the elements needed to renew or reorganize if a major perturbation radically alters structure and function.

Walker et al. (2002) propose an approach to managing resilience in social–ecological systems. Recognizing the high levels of uncertainty in social–ecological systems, they advocate close involvement of stakeholders, so that representatives of stakeholder groups are engaged in establishing the key attributes of the system being studied and the range of possible trajectories that the stakeholders might try to make this system follow. Their four-step framework is thus:

1   Commence with a stakeholder-led development of a conceptual model of the system, including its historical profile (how it got to be what it is)

and preliminary assessments of the drivers that supply key ecosystem goods and services.

2 Identify the range of unpredictable and uncontrollable drivers, stakeholder visions for the future, and contrasting possible future policies, weaving these three factors into a limited set of future scenarios.

3 Having undertaken these steps, then evaluate the social–ecological system for resilience. This will involve, in an iterative manner, developing simple models of the system's dynamics to explore attributes that affect resilience, and undertaking quantitative analyses of elements that determine a system's resilience.

4 Undertake an evaluation of management and policy implications based on input from both scientists and stakeholders.

Given the limits to our understanding of how complex systems behave, Walker et al. focus on learning to live within systems, rather than controlling them. Resilience theorists argue that this can be done by maintaining or increasing the system's resilience. Building resilience comes at a cost, and so should only be undertaken where there is a strong need and in a way that is suited to a particular social–ecological system. Thus, it is important to analyse resilience and enable people to discover how the social–ecological system in which they live might be made more resilient to shocks, and more able to renew or reorganize itself should large shocks occur (Table 3.2). Understanding the loss, creation and maintenance of resilience through the process of co-discovery – by scientists, policy makers, practitioners, stakeholders and citizens – is at the heart of sustainability (Gunderson and Holling, 2002). The goal of resilience management is to prevent a social–ecological system from moving into undesirable configurations, requiring us to understand where resilience resides in the system, and when and how it can be lost or gained.

Conclusion

The cultural landscape is in constant flux, with the rate and direction of change depending on the nature of various change drivers. Forces of change are not always bad; indeed, we can often harness developmental and land management trends to produce interesting new landscapes. However, ill-considered change can disrupt essential linkages within and between social and natural systems, and reduce the capacity of the landscape to adapt to future 'shocks'. Public policies are themselves both change drivers in their own right, and mechanisms to control and deflect changes caused by other social and economic pressures.

Adaptive capacity in a landscape requires building its resilience. Often the resilience is related to physical and ecological systems, and the degree to

Table 3.2 Enabling society to adapt to shocks in the behaviour of cultural landscape systems: an idealized illustration of differences between classical natural resource management theory and ecological resilience theory (summarized from Walker et al., 2002)

Classical natural resource management theory	Ecological resilience theory
Assumes that ecosystem succession moves predictably along an environmental gradient towards a climatic climax ecosystem	In social–ecological systems, the assumption is 'hysteresis', i.e. the possibility of alternative stable states under equal environmental conditions, rather than just one seral or climax stage
Assumes that ecological succession is smooth between seres	The transition between alternative stable states may be subject to thresholds/phase shifts/regime shifts that may be sudden and irreversible rather than gradual and reversible, and discrete rather than continuous
Approaches conditions of rapid environmental change, where key parameters may change faster than we can update information or calculate probability distributions, by focusing on developing more sophisticated predictive models, including decision making under dynamic and unknown probabilities	Approaches conditions of rapid environmental change, not only by drawing upon conventional natural resource management models, but more especially by concentrating on the need to move forward despite vast uncertainties
Accepts that decisions often need to be based on imperfect knowledge, but broadly assumes the relative 'rationality' of actors in relation to the consumption of goods and services	Resilience theorists emphasize 'bounded rationality' of agents, who are not always making and do not always make economically rational or income-maximizing approaches
Assumes that the key probability distributions and utility functions are known	Many important probability distributions are unknown, there are no simple measures of utility or loss that adequately capture all the values of different stakeholders in the system, and some utility functions have not yet been constructed because stakeholders may not know what stakes they hold
Concentrates on improving methods of decision analysis and optimization (e.g. decision support systems, cost–benefit analysis, multi-criteria analysis)	Decision analysis methods do not capture the capacity of people to react to forecasts of future conditions by creating, and acting upon, novel visions of the future; although decision-making models may yield valuable outputs, these are often overridden by the short-termism and pragmatism associated with political cycles

Continued ...

Table 3.2 continued

Classical natural resource management theory	Ecological resilience theory
Resource allocation is based on optimization techniques based on models that make probabilistic predictions	Where actual system behaviour gets too far away from model representation, the predictions fail (this is often because they are so sensitive to initial conditions)
Market imperfections and failure are the exception	Market imperfections are the norm and so market-based valuations are usually distorted
Democratic legitimacy can be represented in models via consumers' preference functions	Agents hold preferences, not just over outcomes (consumption bundles), but over the social, economic and political processes that govern those outcomes, so that most stakeholders are not content to be represented in the process by a mere abstract utility function, and expect more democratic legitimacy
Experts can define the best way forward, subject to public consultation, and markets will regulate resource use reasonably well	Well defined property rights do not exist for many important ecological goods and services and, therefore, markets do not exist. The decision-making process needs to stimulate creative thinking about the future and allow both stakeholders (as an integral component of the social–ecological system) and researchers to compare maps of various pathways to the future. The market will ultimately not sort out the problem of loss of resilience, so that pathways that are robust to ambiguous and unforeseeable changes need to be explored imaginatively in order to increase the resilience of a given social–ecological system

which they are functioning within a desired regime. Equally, it is important to develop social resilience by building up knowledge and capacity at community, organization and government levels. Without innate resilience, a social–ecological system can become brittle and move into a different, and probably less desirable, state.

Building resilience in landscapes requires us to enhance the social, ecological and economic structures and processes that enable it to reorganize following a disturbance. It also requires us to reduce those perturbations that tend to undermine it. However, there remain two major areas that are currently poorly understood. First, we have only a preliminary idea of the thresholds that characterize different types of system, and so our knowledge of the thresholds and tipping points needs to improve, especially if they have not yet been encountered and so remain in the category of 'unknown'. Second, we need to develop a fuller understanding of the rules that govern social–ecological systems as they evolve over time in response to both biophysical and social changes. Understanding this evolution is critical to achieving policies that enable social–ecological systems to self-organize along preferred trajectories. Overall, if we want to ensure the resilient and sustainable functioning of cultural landscapes, they will require sufficient connectivity and space to support their linkages, dynamics, organization and adaptiveness.

Chapter 4

Physical connections in landscapes

Introduction

The physical landscape displays numerous functions, but three in particular operate systemically at the landscape scale, and have been the focus of reconnection programmes – air (particularly urban airspace), water (particularly floodplain management) and land (especially vegetation and habitats). This chapter explores the problems of disconnection and the potentials for reconnection both within and between these physical systems.

Air

The air surrounding us hardly seems like a resource that can be bounded and managed. However, the properties of air, particularly in terms of pollution, have been a substantive policy issue for over a century. The challenges posed by air temperature, especially those associated with global warming, have come to be taken more and more seriously as considerations in spatial planning strategies (Davoudi et al., 2009). Global warming certainly appears to be occurring, with a strong likelihood that it is being caused at least partly by human activities that emit greenhouse gases (GHGs) such as carbon dioxide (CO_2). Whilst the policy solution to this is partly technological and economic – finding ways of driving down GHGs from industrial and domestic processes – some of it is also related to the landscape. On the one hand, tree cover and other vegetation can help us adapt to climate change, especially in areas experiencing urban heat island effects, by making conditions for people, plants and animals more tolerable. On the other hand, it can help to mitigate climate change by acting as a carbon sink.

We have previously noted the need to consider the functionality of cities' airspace. Hotter summers can decrease human comfort, increase heat stress and in extreme cases result in increased mortality. During Europe's notably hot summer of 2003, there were estimated to be up to 35,000 additional deaths as well as more extensive adverse impacts on work productivity and hospital admissions. By 2040, in the UK, probably more than half of summers will be warmer than 2003, and by 2100 summer temperatures similar to 2003 could be classed as cool (Chartered Institution of Water and Environmental Management, 2010). Whilst vegetation may mitigate these effects, it may in turn be limited by diminishing supplies of water and more frequent drought conditions. Hopefully – and this illustrates the importance of interconnections – methods of sustainable water management and alleviation of flood risk can be linked to maintaining functional green space. Reduction of the urban heat island effect can be achieved strategically through the addition of parks and green space, ponds and fountains, and by changing building materials. Vegetation provides shading and cooling through evapotranspiration whilst evaporation from water bodies can have a small but significant cooling effect. Although we should still aim to conserve and create large urban parks, size is not necessarily essential and a considerable amount of cooling can be achieved through the careful planning of green corridors, smaller open spaces, street trees and green roofs. Choice of vegetation in the light of future climatic conditions is also necessary – as green spaces turn brown they no longer exhibit cooling properties, and so species need to be well suited to future climates.

Lafortezza et al. (2009) have studied the ameliorating effect of green spaces on some climatic features, for example their role in providing comfortable outdoor settings for people. Comparing cities in Italy and the UK, they were able to show how people's use of green spaces can alleviate the perception of thermal discomfort during periods of heat stress. It would seem that the shade provided by mature trees can keep surfaces cooler by as much as 15°C in very hot climates. One possible adaptation strategy would be to make greater use of drought-resistant species, particularly locally appropriate drought tolerant trees, as is typical in open spaces in the Mediterranean region. This would require us to improve conditions for street trees so that they have sufficient rooting space and irrigation. New and sustainable types of irrigation in this situation could include rainwater harvesting, reuse of grey water, floodwater storage and using water from urban aquifers where these are rising due to previous cessation of pumping.

Regardless of the success of any future mitigation measures that might be introduced, there will still be some unavoidable carbon-forced climate change as a result of past and present emissions. Consequently, it is advisable to introduce a range of adaptation measures, many of them based on landscape. The Chartered Institution of Water and Environmental Management (2010) noted that UK cities are likely to suffer from increased incidences, severity and duration of heatwaves, flooding and drought. They therefore argue that local authorities and central government should commit to designing new, and adapting old, developments in ways that help to accommodate surface water flooding and attenuate heatwaves, in order to make them more comfortable in future climatic conditions and more resilient to extreme weather. The stresses of climate change will be felt most acutely in urban areas, which are also the most densely populated. Green infrastructure can benefit large numbers of people through the numerous ways in which it can assist urban cooling, wind attenuation and natural drainage. In Stuttgart, Germany, climate-based planning has demonstrated the benefits of a re-connective approach to urban airspace. This has focused on protecting areas where air flow is unimpeded in order to improve air quality and reduce the urban heat island effect. A series of wind paths have been designated across the city that allow cooler mountain air to flow into the heart of the city, and no new building is allowed in an area designated as part of a wind path. The felling of trees of a certain size in inner city areas is banned and, as a result, greenery covers more than 60 per cent of the city. A number of other cities have also established policies that require certain levels of tree planting and green space (Hebbert and Webb, 2011).

Williams et al. (2010) allude to the complementary need to build social resilience. Referring to the situation in suburban areas, they highlight the problems of retrofitting landscape solutions into existing housing stock, where there is very fragmented ownership and management of land and buildings. This is compounded by a very slow rate of land use change, so that there is limited opportunity to design afresh for modern sustainable solutions. The approach therefore needs to emphasize mobilizing social commitment to adaptation, the effective coordination of numerous actors and partnerships, developing political will, generating public acceptance and encouraging changes in people's behaviour.

One of the most comprehensive studies of the connections between green infrastructure and the urban heat island has been by Gill et al. (2007) in Greater Manchester, UK. This analysis utilized an energy exchange and hydrological model, based on surface temperature and surface run-off in relation to the green infrastructure under both current and future climate conditions. The authors characterized the urban environment by mapping urban morphology types (UMTs) followed by a surface cover analysis. The UMTs were a useful proxy for urban landscape types as landscape features are closely related to physical morphology. Each UMT is characterized by distinctive physical features and human activities, and so the researchers could examine links between natural processes and land uses. Broad categories of UMTs were analysed to provide an initial indication of where green patches (e.g. formal and informal open spaces) and green corridors (for example, alongside transport routes) might be found. More precise estimates of green cover within the built matrix were based on a finer-grained analysis of UMT categories, and this revealed that around 72 per cent of the Greater Manchester subregion, or 59 per cent of its 'urbanized' area, consisted of evapotranspiring (i.e. vegetated and water) surfaces. All the UMT categories had, on average, more than 20 per cent evapotranspiring surfaces, but there was huge variation, from 20 per cent in town centres to 98 per cent in woodlands. In general, the proportion of tree cover was fairly low, averaging around 12 per cent of the conurbation, but as

Box 4.1 A summary of landscape intervention effects on an urban climate (based on information in Gill et al., 2007)

Future temperature estimates were based on possible future levels of GHG emissions. Drought effects were simulated by removing the role of grass from the evapotranspiration equations. The model assumed current maximum surface temperature of woodlands to be 18.4°C and of town centres to be 31.2°C. Forecasts suggested these maxima would rise to 19.9°C and 33.2°C by the 2080s (low emissions scenario) or 21.6°C and 35.5°C (high emissions scenario). In high density residential areas, with an evaporating cover of 31 per cent, maximum surface temperatures increased by 1.7–3.7°C by the 2080s; in low density areas, with an evaporating cover of 66 per cent, the increase was 1.4–3.1°C. Adding 10 per cent green cover to areas with little green, such as the town centre and high density residential UMTs kept maximum surface temperatures at or below the 1961–1990 baseline temperatures, except in relation to the 2080s high emissions scenario. By contrast, when 10 per cent green was removed, maximum surface temperatures increased appreciably, adding up to 7–8°C in the most urbanized districts.

Adding green roofs to all buildings had a striking effect on maximum surface temperatures, keeping temperatures below the 1961–1990 level for all time periods and emissions scenarios. Roof greening made the biggest difference in the UMTs where the building proportion is high and the evaporating fraction is low (such as town centres). In contrast, when grass dries and stops evapotranspiring, rivers and canals become the coolest, followed by woodlands.

low as 5 per cent in town centres. Residential areas differed widely in surface cover: in high density residential areas built surfaces (i.e. buildings and other impervious surfaces) covered about two thirds of the area, compared to about half in medium density areas and one third in low density areas. This resulted in average tree coverage of 7 per cent, 13 per cent and 26 per cent respectively. This situation was modelled in order to explore the impact of adding or taking away vegetation in key areas in the conurbation, under a range of future temperature and drought scenarios. The models confirmed the strong relationship between surface temperature and the proportion of green cover (Box 4.1).

Additionally, soil type is very important, with faster infiltrating (e.g. sandy) soils, having lower run-off coefficients than slower infiltrating soils (e.g. clays). The run-off coefficients display the largest range on high infiltration soils and the smallest range on low infiltration soils: thus, as would be expected, surface sealing has a more significant impact on run-off on a sandy soil than on a clay soil. Precipitation, and therefore run-off, is expected to increase significantly by the 2080s. Increasing tree cover did appear to mitigate this effect, although by relatively small amounts that would not be likely to prevent future floods. However, adding green roofs to all the buildings in town centres, retail and high density residential UMTs significantly reduced run-off. This effect became even more pronounced when coupled with sustainable urban drainage techniques.

Table 4.1 Climate adaptation via green infrastructure – an indicative typology (adapted from Gill et al., 2007)

	Corridor	*Patch*	*Matrix*
Flood storage	very important	important	quite important
Infiltration capacity	quite important	important	very important
Evaporative cooling	quite important	very important	important
Shading	quite important	important	very important

Overall, these models suggested that the use of urban green space offers significant potential in moderating the expected effects of climate change, especially the increase in summer temperature and flood hazard. One caveat to the potential of green cover in moderating surface temperatures is the case of a drought, when grass dries out and loses its evaporative cooling function. Forecasts suggest that, in summer, there will be more consecutive dry days as well as heatwaves of longer duration. Thus, it is likely that there will be more cases when the grass loses its evaporative cooling function unless countermeasures are taken. In such situations the role of water surfaces in providing cooling and trees in providing shade become increasingly important.

The effects of urban green on climate amelioration and sustainable drainage also depend on the spatial structure of its connections, patches and matrix (Table 4.1). Thus, green infrastructure has landscape ecological properties – the location and arrangement of corridors, patches and the overall matrix (these are explained more fully in Chapter 5) – that will affect how it performs. For example, in terms of resilience to urban flooding, corridors are particularly important for water storage, yet SuDS (which provide ecological 'patches') also have some importance. For water infiltration, the matrix is especially important, as are patches. Since sandy, faster infiltrating soils are the most effective at reducing surface run-off there may be a case for adapting to climate change through preserving and enhancing vegetated surfaces on such soils, or a case for restricting infill development in lower density residential areas where soils have a high infiltration capacity. Patches of green space, especially larger ones, can develop a distinctive microclimate and, in particular, can assist with evaporative cooling, as well as providing shade. Green space may also reduce the demand for mechanical cooling through air conditioning, which is a contributor to GHGs and, through its emission of waste heat, to the urban heat island effect (Gill et al., 2007).

Water

Over the past century or more, floodplains have been increasingly used for urban development and intensive agriculture, and the need to protect that investment has led to engineered disconnection of the river from its

Figure 4.1 Flooding in the Upper Don Valley, Sheffield

floodplain. A strategic consequence has been a loss of flood attenuation, and increases in flood risk downstream (Figure 4.1).

Landscape change has substantial effects on the regulators of water regimes. These changes may influence flooding from engorged river systems, 'fluvial flooding', and from intense urban rainfall events that overwhelm grey infrastructure, 'pluvial flooding'. Wheater and Evans (2009) report that, in urban areas, vegetated soils are widely replaced with impermeable surfaces, which leads to increased overland flow and reduced infiltration, as the natural storage and attenuation provided by the subsurface is bypassed, and the conveyance of run-off to streams is modified. Often, overland run-off is piped by storm water drainage systems and conveyed rapidly to streams and rivers. The resulting increased and accelerated discharge of run-off can, on the one hand, lead to dramatically increased flood peaks and, on the other, reduced groundwater recharge. The effect of urban development on stream flows depends on the nature of the catchment, with relative effects being greater in areas where natural run-off is low. Natural catchments in temperate latitudes are often most likely to flood after prolonged rainfall in winter, when soils are already wet. By contrast, urban catchments may be relatively unaffected by winter rainfall as they are not so seriously affected by waterlogged soils, but may

Box 4.2 Key reasons for urban flooding associated with grey infrastructure

- Culverts becoming blocked with litter and vegetation, washed into them during heavy rainfall events.
- Increased risk of pluvial flooding from surface water run-off due to the vast and diverse extent of impermeable surfaces.
- Ageing and inadequate sewage systems may cause foul sewers to overflow, block natural flow paths or increase run-off rates.
- Residential drains have typically been designed to cope with a one in thirty year flood occurrence, which is likely to prove inadequate in light of climate change projections for the future.

be seriously affected by intense summer rainfall (pluvial flooding). The magnitude of this change is complex, however, and varies according to such factors as location of the urban area within the river catchment and size of the catchment.

In urban areas, grey infrastructure usually channels storm run-off via gully pots into storm sewers which are designed to accommodate relatively frequent events. Under more extreme conditions, these sewers will start to surcharge (flow full under pressure) and, as pressures build up, they may discharge to the surface. Such flows combine with surface run-off to generate flooding of roads and properties. These problems are typically exacerbated by sewer blockages and other failures (Box 4.2).

In recent years, serious flooding associated with the main European rivers, such as the Rhine, has led to some changes of approach. Thus, in some cities, there has been a significant decrease in the levels of flood protection, accompanied by a new focus on recreating floodplain storage. As noted previously, in The Netherlands there has been a move towards 'Living with Water' rather than simply trying to control water by conventional civil and municipal engineering techniques. Hence, there is a growing interest in the possibility of reverting some floodplain land to an active water storage role, for example by reducing the level of flood protection on selected low-lying farmland.

A key unknown in relation to flooding is the effect of future climate change. Bartens (2009) has reviewed the situation in the UK, and notes the broad expectation that temperatures will increase in winter and summer, compounded by more extreme summer heatwaves. Winters will become wetter with more days of rain and more volume of precipitation, with worst-case estimates suggesting that flood risk could rise by 200 per cent. Sea level pressure will be higher during winter months, coinciding with anticipated heavier rainfalls. Northern areas are expected to rise while southern areas will sink. Overall, therefore, risks will vary across the country – some areas will face a bigger risk from coastal flooding, some from fluvial flooding and some from pluvial flooding. About 10 per cent of houses in England are built

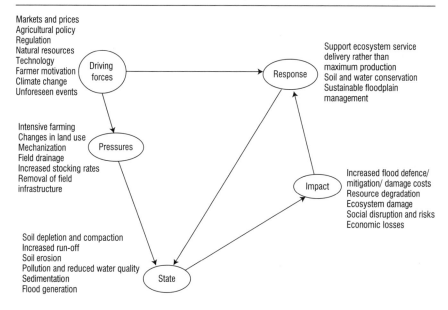

Markets and prices
Agricultural policy
Regulation
Natural resources
Technology
Farmer motivation
Climate change
Unforeseen events

Driving forces

Response

Support ecosystem service
delivery rather than
maximum production
Soil and water conservation
Sustainable floodplain
management

Intensive farming
Changes in land use
Mechanization
Field drainage
Increased stocking rates
Removal of field
infrastructure

Pressures

Impact

Increased flood defence/
mitigation/ damage costs
Resource degradation
Ecosystem damage
Social disruption and risks
Economic losses

Soil depletion and compaction
Increased run-off
Soil erosion
Pollution and reduced water quality
Sedimentation
Flood generation

State

Figure 4.2 A DPSIR model of flood generation in agricultural landscapes (based on O'Connell et al., 2004)

on a floodplain and, since the year 2000, 11 per cent of new homes have been built in flood hazard areas.

Looking at rural rivers, O'Connell et al. (2004) used the DPSIR model (Figure 4.2) to relate changes in run-off generation regimes to various land management practices, notably the intensification of farming and forestry that has occurred over the past fifty years or so. The authors found a large body of evidence indicating that, in the long term, afforestation reduces flows due to increased evaporation, particularly in relation to coniferous and upland forests, although some drainage practices have tended to increase storm run-off for considerable periods. Agricultural drainage can also have substantial effects on flooding. The use of underground pipe systems to drain soils to improve production is a widespread agricultural practice, and very low-permeability soils have often been subjected to a secondary treatment such as 'subsoiling' or 'moling' to improve the flow of water to field drains. Although dependent on a range of local factors, the installation of field drains generally causes a reduction in surface and near-surface run-off due to a lowering of the water table and an increase in the available storage capacity of the soil. Some flooding is also attributable to agricultural intensification, particularly where hedgerows have been extensively removed, field sizes greatly increased, land drains run down steep slopes, and riparian vegetation completely removed so that intensive farming continues right up to the straightened channel edges. With regard to the disruption of the riparian zone, noted above, Burt and Pinay (2005) found that channel–floodplain linkage – or the 'bank storage' effect created at the river–wetland interface – had a particularly significant role in reducing diffuse pollution from agricultural nitrogen loads.

These landscape practices have often been accompanied by intensification of production. In the uplands, there has been an increase in the amount of improved pasture – which entails draining, ploughing and reseeding – and this often affects the source areas of river catchments. Further, this marginal land has often been subject to overgrazing due to increased numbers of sheep. The degradation of soil structure, which may arise on arable land from heavy machinery and on pasture from overgrazing, can result in reduced soil infiltration rates and available storage capacities, which in turn will accelerate run-off in the form of overland flow. Whilst catchment-scale effects of land use and land management changes have proved difficult to evaluate there is considerable evidence that optimally placed shelterbelts and woodlands could reduce flood peaks, as well as helping to reduce diffuse pollution and improve wildlife habitats (O'Connell et al., 2004).

In addition to understanding the generation of run-off from fields and hill slopes, and how this affects the amount and timing of water entering rivers, there is also the question of how the flows affect areas downstream. A key issue has been the disconnection of rivers from their floodplains, particularly arising from engineered flood protection for agricultural land. There has been a recent trend away from this defence mentality of protection for farms in floodplains, by seeking to reduce flood risk downstream through the re-establishment of natural storage and attenuation of water associated with floodplain inundation. This is not always appropriate as some agricultural areas with flood defences may act as washlands in high flows, so effects on the catchment must be carefully judged. Deliberately increasing flood risk to farms also raises some very sensitive social and economic issues, such as the distress of losing crops and the disadvantageous position of tenant farmers. The issue is clearly one of building social resilience as much as physical resilience.

Turning to urban rivers, the impact of climate change on flooding is likely to be particularly noticeable in urban areas, with rainfall intensities rising by up to 40 per cent by 2080 and the costs of defending these areas increasing several times over (Chartered Institution of Water and Environmental Management, 2010). In the past the solution to flooding in most urban areas has been to straighten rivers and contain them in channels and culverts, but this tends to speed up river flow and increase peak flows. By contrast, un-engineered rivers with vegetated channels slow down flows and tend to channel water to natural floodplains thereby avoiding flooding in built up areas. Within the urban fabric itself, we previously noted the increasingly widespread use of SuDS, whose principle is based on controlling flow rates near to the source through a mixture of permeable surfaces, filters, storage areas, wetlands and balancing ponds that help to minimize surface water run-off, protect water quality and provide habitats for wildlife (Box 4.3).

Box 4.3 Some benefits of SuDS (based on Environment Agency, 2008)

SuDS offer a combination of benefits that conventional drainage systems do not provide, such as:

- protection and enhancement of water quality and biodiversity in local streams;
- protection and restoration of riparian vegetation;
- improvement of amenities for recreational purposes, in contrast to the unsightliness of large concrete structures;
- maintenance or restoration of the natural flow regime in streams;
- protection of people and property from flooding, now and in the future;
- protection of watercourses from pollution caused by accidental spillages and misconnections;
- allowing new development in areas where sewerage systems are already at full capacity, encouraging new development within existing developed areas and protecting greenfield sites;
- incorporating designs that are sympathetic to their environmental setting and the needs of the community;
- allowing natural groundwater recharge where this is considered appropriate;
- reducing the cost of hard structures such as roadside kerbs and gullies, and also of their related maintenance.

As urban development intensifies, ground becomes more extensively sealed, natural drainage patterns are disrupted, and so more surface water runs rapidly into rivers and less filters through the soil (Environment Agency, 2008). Traditional grey infrastructure is designed to remove rainfall from these impervious surfaces as quickly as possible. This causes higher flow rates for shorter periods (Figure 4.3) and can result in flooding further downstream, as well as increased riverbank and riverbed erosion with consequential damage to riparian habitat and downstream deposition of sediment and debris. The increase in impermeable areas that accompanies development also results in less water being available for infiltration into the ground. This can reduce the volume of water stored in the ground, lowering groundwater levels and reducing the amount of groundwater available to feed into streams and rivers. SuDS are based on an alternative approach to surface water management, namely, keeping water on site longer, by endeavouring to mimic the natural movement of water from a development, reducing flood risk, improving water quality and reducing diffuse pollution.

The 'hard' engineering approach has thus aimed to use barriers designed to cope with known levels of peak flow and system capacity. SuDS work on equally rigorous engineering principles but aim to build environmental resilience by reconnecting hydrological systems and mimicking nature in the surface water management process (Environment Agency, 2008). In addition, social resilience may need to be increased, so that people more readily accept minor flood risk, such as allowing shallow flooding of a car

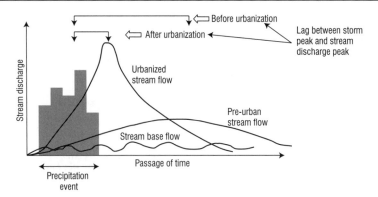

Figure 4.3 Effect of urbanization on water discharge peaks (based on Christopherson, 1997)

park for short periods once or twice a year rather than building a much larger drainage system to cater for such infrequent events. There are three main SuDS options, which in practice often overlap, namely: reduce the quantity of run-off from the site (source control techniques); slow the velocity of run-off to allow settlement filtering and infiltration (permeable conveyance systems); and provide passive treatment to surface water that has collected in SuDS before its discharge into groundwater or to a watercourse (end of pipe systems).

Urban blue–green infrastructure can be integrated through a three-dimensional approach, or 'stacking', which reflects the connectivities between above-ground, ground-level and below-ground elements. Thus, green roofs can be used to reduce the volume and rate of run-off so that downstream SuDS and other drainage infrastructure can be reduced in size. 'Hard landscape' materials such as permeable pavements made of gravel, grasscrete, porous concrete blocks or porous asphalt may be used in place of traditional pavements. Sometimes they may need to be accompanied by subsurface storage spaces that enable reuse or delayed discharge of the water. Rainwater may be harvested from roofs and hard surfaces such as car parks, and can be stored and used in and around properties. Shallow, excavated and suitably lined infiltration trenches will allow storm water run-off from small catchments to gradually infiltrate into the subsoil. Larger areas can be similarly served by infiltration basins, which incorporate more extensive surface storage of storm water. Below ground, a structural soil with high porosity (e.g. crushed concrete), sometimes planted with suitable vegetation, can serve to improve infiltration rates of run-off volume (Melby and Cathcart, 2002; Bartens, 2009). Of course, SuDS need careful design, construction and regular maintenance; they may not always provide complete solutions and may need back-up with more conventional elements to cope with major events.

Small-scale systems such as filter strips – vegetated sections of land designed to accept run-off as overland sheet flow – can be designed into landscaped areas and are sited upstream of other SuDS. Large-scale, 'end of pipe' systems usually involve storage of water in constructed ponds where natural purification processes can be encouraged. Constructed wetlands and ponds also provide the opportunity to improve wildlife habitat in urban areas, as well as amenity. Detention basins are designed to hold back the 'first flush' of storm run-off for a few hours to allow solids to settle; they drain into a watercourse or surface water drainage system and are dry outside storm periods. Retention ponds, by contrast, retain a certain volume of water at all times, thus avoiding the unsightly exposure of banks of collected sediment, and assisting the process of removing nutrients, trace metals, coliforms and organic matter. Allowance for a considerable variation in water level during storms is incorporated in the design, so that a significant storage volume can still be provided. If retention ponds have a catchment of at least 5 hectares and/or a reliable inflow of water in dry weather, they are also likely to perform well as amenity features. Ponds can be fed by a swale system, a filter drain network or, if a sufficiently large area can be provided to accommodate peak flows, a conventional surface water system. A typical retention pond will have at least twenty days retention time to permit biological degradation of pollutants. Overall, the ecosystem services provided by blue infrastructure facilities are summarized in Table 4.2.

In the US, there has been widespread use of 'watershed forestry' to help reconnect and regulate water flows in both rural and urban areas. Its key elements are:

- protect – for example using conservation easements and ordinances to require developers to protect selected forests during construction;
- enhance – promoting the enhancement of health, condition and function of urban forest fragments;
- reforest – reforesting open land through natural regeneration or new planting.

Whilst such approaches obviously have costs associated with them, they also have major benefits. For example, a study by the Philadelphia Parks Alliance (Trust for Public Land, 2008) reports that the NGO American Forests analysed the ecosystem services of urban trees in terms of reducing storm water run-off, improving air quality, saving summer energy, and carbon sequestration and avoidance. It illustrated the value of urban trees in relation to the Baltimore–Washington area, where tree cover was estimated to have declined from 51 per cent to 37 per cent between 1973 and 1997. This reduction was linked to a 19 per cent increase in storm water run-off and consequential new storm water treatment systems to intercept this run-

Table 4.2 The nature and function of blue infrastructure (based on Bartens, 2009)

| Issue | Blue infrastructure properties | | |
	Function	Type	Location
Fluvial flooding	Increased drainage area, reducing drainage to sewers and streams	→ Pervious surfaces, coarse-grained soils	→ Floodplains, land adjacent to watercourses, low-lying and potentially waterlogged land
	Reduced peak flow rate, reducing flooding and bank erosion	→ Trees/roots to intercept/help infiltration, detention reservoirs to collect water	→ Floodplains, wetlands, areas upstream of vulnerable land
	Water storage to protect critical flood risk areas	→ Detention/retention ponds, wetlands, rain gardens/bioretention	→ Floodplains, high rainfall areas, areas with many impervious surfaces, areas upstream of vulnerable land
	Removal of surplus water and rainfall interception	→ Evaporation from leaf surfaces, uptake by trees and plants, green roofs	→ Floodplains, high rainfall areas, areas upstream of vulnerable land
	Soil infiltration	→ Roots of all plants, especially trees	
Pluvial flooding	Increased pervious area leading to reduced run-off and floodwater	→ Pervious surfaces, coarse-grained soils	→ Floodplains, areas of heavy rainfall, areas close to frequently overflowing sewers, low-lying and potentially waterlogged land
	Reduced rate and volume of water to sewers	→ Store water in designed depressions, use trees to intercept and impede	→ Close to impervious surfaces
	Removal of surplus rainfall and interception to reduce run-off	→ Trees, especially large ones, and green roofs	→ Within and upstream of vulnerable land, floodplains and areas of high precipitation, low-lying and potentially waterlogged areas

	Drainage area to reduce floodwater	→ Wider pervious area results in better drainage, vegetation improves soil infiltration	→ Within the buffer and in vulnerable land
	Water loss and reduced flow rate or ingress	→ Uptake by plants/trees and evapotranspiration from leaf surfaces, detention and interception	→ Within the buffer, vulnerable land, floodplains, water collection and conveyance areas
Water quantity and quality	Water storage (increase)	→ Ponds	→ Areas of high precipitation and high stream flow
	Evaporation (decrease)	→ Shading by vegetation	→ All water bodies, especially smaller ones
	Reducing peak flow rates in order to reduce bank erosion and sedimentation	→ Water storage in designed depressions, using vegetation to impede and intercept water	→ Areas of high precipitation, wetlands, and water collection and conveyance areas
	Reduced pollution load by uptake and adsorption	→ Uptake by vegetation, adsorption by soils (including structural soils)	→ Variety of urban and rural land uses

off; further, this lost tree cover would, if it had remained, have removed approximately 4.23 million kilograms of pollutants from the atmosphere annually. At 1999 prices, the capital cost of this additional storm water treatment and annual cost of pollutant removal were estimated at US$1.08 billion and US$24 million respectively.

In sum, we can conclude that the benefits of reconnected blue infrastructure include flood attenuation, water quality improvement, recreation, evaporative cooling, biodiversity, community value and amenity. It should also be noted that, with inappropriate design or plant selection, they may be associated with pollution hotspots, uptake of space, possible backing up of water, health hazards, uptake of scarce water during seasonal drought and poor aesthetics. Further, coniferous trees will tend to give year-round benefits whereas some of the benefits of deciduous trees will only be experienced during the growing season. More ambitious reconnection of watercourses may provide ways for aquatic species to bypass natural biogeographic barriers to colonization: sometimes this may be good, but on occasion it may have negative consequences by allowing invasive species to spread or by exposing endemics to new competitors. As with all attempts at landscape reconnection, therefore, design and management should always be based on a sound appreciation of nature.

Land

Terrestrial reconnections mainly centre on creating space for biodiversity, particularly by expanding and linking habitats, so that keystone species can maintain demographically and genetically viable populations. In this respect, the debate about habitat conservation has shifted significantly away from one of protecting high quality patches (although site safeguard remains a lynchpin of an effective conservation strategy) towards a new 'restorative' approach that rebuilds nature through ecological networks. Three key drivers of biodiversity change – habitat loss, habitat deterioration and eutrophication – have led to new nature conservation strategies that aim to create a more resilient natural environment, with new space for nature (Lawton et al., 2010).

A highly influential review of nature conservation policy in England (Lawton et al., 2010) examined whether present wildlife protection sites comprised a coherent and resilient ecological network and, if not, what needed to be done. Whilst there were some positive recent signals in the recovery of biodiversity, this was often because the more adaptable generalist species were faring quite well, whereas the more specialist species tended to be in decline. This indicated a continuing problem of environmental quality and variety, in large part because improvements in key wildlife habitats had been offset by those habitats becoming increasingly fragmented and isolated. The Lawton Review thus recommended an approach based on restoring species and habitats to sustainable levels (in a context of changing climate)

Box 4.4 Effects of climate change on species and habitats (based on Hopkins, 2009; Lawton et al., 2010)

- Range change – all species have a 'climate envelope' within which they can survive and reproduce, and outside of which they die. As the climate changes, these climate envelopes move, so that species will need to track these movements and occupy new areas. At present, in the UK, warmth loving southern species are expanding their range northwards or uphill and some cold-adapted northern species are retreating at their southern limit of their distribution. There has also been a natural spread of new species. It is unclear how long these observed patterns of change will continue. Species will not automatically track changes in the climate, either because they are poor dispersers, prevented from dispersing by hostile barriers in the environment, or because other essential components of their environment such as specific food supplies or breeding sites fail to keep pace with climate change.
- Phenological (seasonal event) change – in the UK, there are now some clear effects, such as the first leafing dates of trees, the flight times of moths and butterflies, egg-laying dates for birds, the first spawning of amphibians, the first appearance of hoverflies and the fruiting times of species such as blackberry. Differential changes in these seasonal events (loss of synchronization) can cause serious problems for some species because crucial links in food chains are disrupted. Examples include a mismatch between peak caterpillar abundance and the food-needs of nestling woodland birds, and between flowering times and pollinator emergence. In the future such mismatches could disrupt the functioning, persistence and resilience of many ecosystems and have a major impact on ecosystem services.
- Changing habitat preferences – some species have, for example, begun to breed in a wider range of habitats. Whilst it is difficult to generalize, these changes may be beneficial to rare species.
- Sea level rise – changing sea levels caused partly by climate change have already led to loss of intertidal habitat, particularly on the low-lying coasts of south-east England where significant losses of saltmarsh have been recorded from key sites. The problem is likely to get worse.

and restoring and securing the long-term sustainability of key ecological and physical processes. This was combined with a desire to promote the role of biodiversity management as part of the wider pursuit of improving ecosystem services, and making wildlife sites more publicly accessible.

Of all the various change drivers affecting wildlife, the Lawton Review suggested that climate change, particularly in the longer term, may have the most serious impact. Already, several climatically related changes are occurring such as shifts in species ranges and changes in the timing of seasonal events. Not all changes will be harmful, but, in the longer term some species may struggle to survive, and other impacts such as sea level rise, an increase in extreme weather events and prolonged summer droughts are likely to have broadly negative effects (Box 4.4). For example, it has been estimated that by 2050, 15–37 per cent of terrestrial plants and animals worldwide could be 'committed to extinction' due to climate change (Thomas et al.,

2004). Establishing a coherent and resilient ecological network would help wildlife to cope with these changes, and improve the ability of the natural environment to provide a range of high quality ecosystem services. It could also assist our response to climate change by, for example, storing carbon or improving the security of water supplies, and by keeping a range of options open in the face of future uncertainty.

Habitat networks, which lie at the heart of this more strategic approach, generally begin with an existing top tier of high value, strongly protected sites, and then extend their coverage through newly created sites. Increasing site connectivity is also important, though it has little benefit unless there are high quality sites with thriving wildlife populations to connect. Local circumstances are also important – thus, in areas that have large amounts of relatively unfragmented habitat, the best strategy will often be to focus on improving management and enhancing habitat diversity ('heterogeneity'), whereas in areas that only have small and isolated sites, it will be better to invest in the restoration and creation of new wildlife habitat. In addition, the need to enhance and extend additional tiers of sites has led to official measures in the UK to introduce Nature Improvement Areas for the purposes of landscape-scale ecological restoration. Since recreating large expanses of continuous natural habitat is not a feasible option in most developed countries, an alternative approach is to secure a suite of high quality sites that collectively – as an ecological network – contain the range and area of habitats that species require and ensure that ecological connections exist to allow species, or at least their genes, to move between them. It is this network of core sites connected by other elements that are important in their own right and can also act as 'stepping stones' – buffer zones, wildlife corridors and small high quality sites – that is referred to as an *ecological network*. As Hilty et al. (2006) have shown, 'wildlife corridors' do not have to be physically continuous, and a mosaic of mixed land use will often perform equally satisfactorily.

The Lawton Review set out five attributes against which such a network could be assessed: (1) the network should support the full range of a country's biodiversity and incorporate ecologically important areas; (2) the network and its component sites should be of adequate size, taking account of the need to adapt to climate change; (3) the network sites need long-term protection and appropriate management; (4) sufficient ecological connections should exist between sites to enable species movement; and (5) sites should be valued by, and accessible to, people. Given that many species are now largely restricted to wildlife sites simply because they have mostly been lost from everywhere else, the future need is thus to rebuild nature. The Review distilled the essence of a more resilient and coherent ecological network as – *more*, *bigger*, *better* and *joined*. This requires action to improve the quality of current sites by better habitat management, increasing their size, enhancing connections between them either through physical corridors

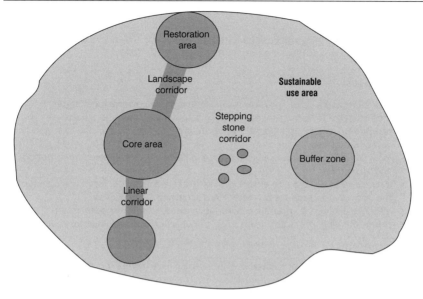

Figure 4.4 Idealized elements of an ecological network (based on Bennett and Mulongoy, 2006)

or 'stepping stones', creating new sites, and reducing the pressures on wildlife by improving the wider environment.

As well as linking down to local component networks, linkage can also be upwards, and there are currently more than 250 ecological networks planned or being established at regional, national and international levels around the world (Jongman et al., 2011; Jongman and Pungetti, 2004; Bennett and Mulongoy, 2006). Different approaches to ecological networks reflect differences between countries in the extent of their remaining natural habitats, the needs of their focal species, and countries' planning and policy systems. In countries where population pressure and development are relatively light, wilderness areas may be the focus of the networks. By contrast, in Western Europe the most important areas are often semi-natural habitats on relatively small sites that already enjoy a high level of protection and where the purpose is to improve the ecological connections between sites and restore lost habitats. Despite these differences, a number of elements consistently characterize ecological networks (Bennett and Mulongoy, 2006): a focus on conserving wild plants and animals at the landscape, ecosystem or regional scale; an emphasis on maintaining or strengthening ecological coherence, primarily by increasing connectivity with corridors and 'stepping stones'; ensuring that critical areas are buffered from the effects of potentially damaging external activities; restoring degraded ecosystems and ecological processes; and promoting the sustainable use of natural resources in areas of importance to wildlife (Figure 4.4; Box 4.5).

Box 4.5 Key principles and components of an ecological network (based on Bennett and Mulongoy, 2006; Hopkins, 2009; Lawton et al., 2010)

Principles:

- clear aims and a vision, possibly including quantified performance targets;
- local stakeholder engagement, including landowners, from the outset;
- promotion, where appropriate, of multifunctional use of the network and its component sites;
- local flexibility in delivery to reflect local differences in implementation options and aspirations;
- a sound evidence base, to ensure the right sites are included, for management of the network, and to assess whether it is achieving its objectives;
- effective protection of all the network components, not just core areas;
- proper funding, preferably from a mix of public, private and voluntary sources.

Components:

- Core areas – well protected and possessing high nature conservation value, forming the heart of the network, and from which healthy breeding populations of species can disperse to other parts of the network. These contain habitats that are rare or important because of the wildlife they support or the ecosystem services they provide, and generally have the highest concentrations of species or support rare species.
- Corridors and 'stepping stones' – spaces that improve the functional connectivity between core areas, enabling species to move between them to feed, disperse, migrate or reproduce. Connectivity need not come from linear, continuous habitats, but more often arises from a land 'mosaic' where a number of small sites act as 'stepping stones' across which certain species can move between core areas. Specific corridors such as under- and overpasses may be needed where the dispersal of target species (e.g. flightless mammals) is impeded by barriers such as major road networks.
- Restoration areas – where measures are planned to restore or create new habitat so that ecological functions and species populations can be restored. They are often situated so as to complement, connect or enhance existing core areas.
- Buffer zones – areas that closely surround core areas, restoration areas, 'stepping stones' and ecological corridors, and protect them from the adverse impacts from the wider environment.
- Sustainable use areas – areas within the wider landscape whose use is based on sustainable land management and related economic activity (Bennett and Mulongoy, 2006). Set up appropriately, they help to 'soften the matrix' outside the network and make it more permeable and less hostile to wildlife, including self-sustaining populations of species that are dependent upon, or at least tolerant of, certain forms of agriculture.

One of the difficulties of promoting habitat networks, relative to focusing on the protection of particular habitats and species, is that the approach needs to be based on generalizations about ecological processes. We cannot be precise about the appropriate size and connectivity of all protected sites

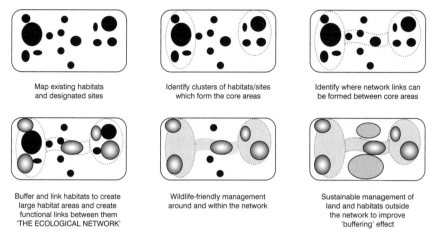

Map existing habitats and designated sites	Identify clusters of habitats/sites which form the core areas	Identify where network links can be formed between core areas
Buffer and link habitats to create large habitat areas and create functional links between them 'THE ECOLOGICAL NETWORK'	Wildlife-friendly management around and within the network	Sustainable management of land and habitats outside the network to improve 'buffering' effect

Figure 4.5 Progressive development of a hypothetical landscape network (adapted from Living Landscape for South East, Kent Wildlife Trust et al., 2006)

because species of plants and animals differ enormously in the size of their home ranges, seed-dispersal distances, population densities, ability to cross hostile landscapes, and so on. Since these cannot all be known or modelled, conservation managers need more broadly to concentrate on measures that increase system resilience, by stabilizing declining populations and enhancing the abundances and distributions of as many as possible. Thus, it is often suggested that we need to concentrate on the overall 'direction of travel', rather than trying to be unrealistically precise about the exact extent and spatial properties of an ecological network.

In order to ensure species survival in the face of climate change, Hopkins (2009) suggests ensuring an element of redundancy in protected-area series and other conservation networks, as this provides insurance in the face of uncertain climate change impacts. As well as incorporating extensive rural areas, networks would need to include more urban habitats because of declines in species with highly anthropogenic associations (e.g. house sparrow *Passer domesticus*). However, it is not just dispersal but also the establishment and breeding success at new sites that is critical to restoring connectivity. Thus the ecological quality of habitat patches, not just their spatial arrangement, is important. An approach to achieving appropriate spatial and qualitative properties in a conservation network is illustrated by the 'Living Landscapes' strategy of the UK non-governmental wildlife conservation trusts (Kent Wildlife Trust et al., 2006) (Figure 4.5).

Some of the most interesting recent work on ecological reconnection has been through the development of Forest Habitat Networks (FHN). Studies suggest that the new or improved woodlands in these networks do not always need to be physically connected with existing woodland, but that woodland species will disperse across small distances of the matrix between existing and new habitat patches. Options in these networks have been identified as: using broadleaved woodland specialist networks to identify where to prioritize efforts; protecting and consolidating high biodiversity woods with buffered expansion; following this up by selecting lower quality woods for targeted improvement; introducing stepping stones to reduce woodland fragmentation; and possibly converting some conifer woods to broadleaved ones where it will reduce broadleaved fragmentation.

For example, a regional analysis of south-west Scotland (Grieve et al., 2006), built on an earlier national mapping exercise of networks for woodland generalists, broadleaved woodland specialists and heathland generalists. The study identified the quantity and location of the broadleaved woodland specialist networks, the quantity and location of high quality broadleaved woodlands within these, the species that rely on these networks, and the nature of regional constraints to lowland woodland expansion. The analysis used the generic focal species approach (Watts et al., 2005) to group woodlands that share several required habitat characteristics, and also considered the permeability to species in other types of land cover. People familiar with the woodlands were asked to evaluate biodiversity quality characteristics of individual woodland blocks so that each polygon could be categorized as good, moderate or poor, with the first of these qualifying as high biodiversity core areas. The model was then supplemented with data on the permeability of each land cover type for broadleaved woodland specialists and on approximate dispersal ranges for the broadleaved woodland specialists, in order to identify existing and potential functional linkages. The model identified possible habitat networks and potential stepping stones that, if acted upon, could provide a basis for targeting grant schemes for management and woodland expansion.

Conclusion

The major systems of the physical landscape – air, water and land – have been widely disrupted through urban and rural development. Losses of critical linkages have reduced their functionality and their capacity to adapt to changing conditions. Understanding the effects of structural disconnection can help us to develop regenerative design approaches that combine economic growth and liveability with environmental integrity. This chapter has reviewed the major physical systems operating in the landscape, and their role in maintaining what are sometimes referred to as 'Goldilocks conditions' – just right for human habitation and current biodiversity, for example, neither too hot nor too cold (Figure 4.6).

Our atmosphere and climatic space has been adversely impacted by the effects of industry and urbanization. This is increasingly serious in the light of climate change. In addition to induced ecological change, increases in

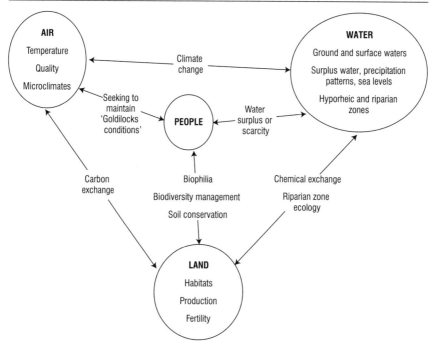

Figure 4.6 Key areas of connectivities between natural systems and their links to people

global temperature may cause serious human discomfort in many major cities. There is already widespread evidence of the effect of temperature change on flooding. Whilst these problems are being partly addressed by technological approaches to carbon reduction, the landscape has a major role to play. Connected landscape strategies can absorb atmospheric carbon and create opportunities that encourage lower-carbon lifestyles. They can also make conditions more liveable, given the climate impacts that will inevitably take place.

Surface and groundwater systems of town, countryside and coast have been disrupted through the replacement of soft natural surfaces by hard artificial ones. By and large, this has served us well for many decades, and often continues to do so. However, there is increasing evidence that 'engineered disconnection' has created unsustainable drainage patterns. Modern design practices confirm that there is no need for a wholesale return to natural drainage patterns but, rather, that smart solutions can enable us to lead modern and prosperous lifestyles whilst still enabling water flows to recover their lost connectivities.

The loss of network connections in ecosystems has received a great deal of attention from scientists. There is a widespread acceptance that traditional nature conservation approaches, based on protection of key sites, are necessary but not sufficient. Consequently, many ecological networks have now been established around the world. The components of effective ecological networks are now widely agreed. However, we are involved in a race against time to ensure that the creation of effective landscape-scale networks in town, country and urban fringe can match the pace of species extinction.

Understanding the physical basis of landscape-scale disconnection is only one side of the argument. Whilst scientific and engineering solutions may be well articulated, there is an equal need to ensure the social, political and economic support to effect their implementation. Almost all of the measures to reconnect physical landscape systems will be highly controversial. People may be required to accept higher levels of flood hazard, change their land management practices, tolerate the survival and even reintroduction of species that damage livestock and crops, and accept the loss in value of potentially developable urban sites. There are many other ways in which the promotion of long-term landscape resilience will restrain short-term human preferences or economic opportunity. Hence, we need to build social capacity through a process of shared learning if regenerative designs are to be accepted. The following chapter considers the links between society and landscape, which underpin our likelihood of making the necessary physical innovations.

Chapter 5

Social connections in landscapes

Introduction

Whilst nature needs 'space' it could be argued that people need 'place'. People connect with landscape in a number of ways. It is claimed, for example, that various landscape qualities and properties lead to attachment to or identification with a place, and may promote social inclusion by creating venues for encounters and shared activities. Pleasant landscapes evidently contribute to people's health and well-being both as restorative settings for mental and spiritual replenishment and as places for more energetic exercise. Enrolling people in the intelligent care of landscape, whether as part of their livelihood or for reasons of fulfilment and enjoyment, can help foster awareness of environmental dynamics and sensitivities, and of our responsibilities towards nature. There is some evidence that the landscape provides an arena in which social learning can occur and institutional thickness can develop, both through direct involvement in land care and through wider engagement in collaborative and participatory governance of environmental programmes (Schusler et al., 2003). Finally, there are demonstrable links between landscape quality and economic sustainability, both because the landscape can be an attractive setting for investment (Henneberry et al., 2004; Rowley et al., 2008) and because valued cultural landscapes have acquired many of their distinctive qualities as accidental by-products of economic activity.

A key issue concerns the lack of good quality landscape resources in areas where most people live. For instance, in the UK, over 80 per cent of the population live in urban settlements and this has recently been associated with 'densification' – the average building density of new dwellings in England rose from twenty-five to forty-four dwellings per hectare in the first decade of the twenty-first century. Urban sprawl and 'edge cities' extend these pressures over wider areas. Green space is often least available in areas where it is most needed. Studies have found that vegetation, and in particular tree cover, tends to be lower in neighbourhoods where there are higher levels of socio-economic deprivation (Pauleit et al., 2003). These areas will be least able to adapt to climate change whilst a lack of green space compounds their disproportionate levels of health deprivation. Overall, there is a strong case for introducing green infrastructure into places where people live.

Connecting people with place

It has been widely suggested that one of the benefits of urban green infrastructure is its contribution to sense of place and community identity. Clarke (2010) has summarized the reasons why this is assumed to be the case. Significantly, the distribution of socially excluded areas often coincides with sparse green space of poor quality; studies in UK cities indicate that in deprived inner-city areas, trees and green space only constitute 2 per cent of land, whereas in wealthy areas they make up 10 per cent. In high density urban areas public space, of good quality, is needed for social interaction and community satisfaction. Perceived quality relates to good access, cleanliness, aesthetics and presence of wildlife, and it has been suggested that these potentially contribute to pride in place and a reduction in antisocial behaviour. Community involvement in the design and management of green infrastructure may promote types of stewardship that can lead to reduced management costs and a reduced need to repair vandalism over the long term. Creating a strong place identity can benefit the social vibrancy of communities and individuals, whilst green space can play a role in producing feelings of attachment towards the wider community. Other research points to the role of the landscape itself, and its associated time-depth and cultural signatures, in creating a distinctive locality with which people identify (Figure 5.1).

The Millennium Ecosystem Assessment (MEA) noted that we rely on the environment for a range of 'cultural services', and these bear a strong relationship to the experiential qualities of landscape. One study (Natural England, 2009a) considered eight cultural landscape services, based on the MEA list, namely – sense of history or heritage, sense of place or identity, inspiration or stimulus, calm and tranquillity, leisure and recreational activities, spiritual value, learning and education, and the sense of escapism associated with getting away from it all (Box 5.1). Clearly, the experience of landscape is a very holistic or integrated matter that is not easily disaggregated into different 'services'. Nonetheless, the study did succeed in gathering evidence about the nature of these services and in relating their occurrence to particular landscape components. For example, one theme related to landscape as a setting to find peace and solitude, as well as exercise and activity. People referred to a sense of escape and stress relief, and the opportunity to spend time with loved ones or to be alone. Complementing this was a life-affirming experience of physical sensation, such as sound, silence or 'the wind in your hair'. People's experiences varied in intensity, ranging from special places that deliver strong emotions, to more mundane

Figure 5.1 Lindisfarne Island, UK: a key example of a landscape possessing great time-depth and cultural resonances, which combine with highly distinctive physical qualities (photo: Jill Selman)

areas that still deliver day-to-day opportunities for contact with nature. People often had a portfolio of places they would access for different types of experience, including somewhere nearby and easily accessible such as a local park or riverbank, and somewhere a bit further away but more varied, typically having a combination of features, such as woodland, fields and water. There would often be very special places that were well known and popular, such as a distinctive hill, but people would also have secret places that few others knew about and which provided them with greater solitude or the opportunity for special activities such as birdwatching. As the authors of the study observed, it seemed that modern living creates a degree of 'sensory deprivation' that can be countered by the experience of landscape.

Although people tended to talk about 'whole landscape' experiences, certain elements proved to be particularly recurrent. For example, water, in its various forms, greatly enhanced people's landscape experience, often complementing the beauty or tranquillity of a place. The presence of water was often a focal point or a linking aspect that added symmetry to the landscape experience, amplified the effectiveness of landscape in delivering many cultural benefits, and had a therapeutic aspect. Moving, rushing water was exhilarating, still water was peaceful, and water in a marshland was valued for its wildlife capacity. The sound of water was often mentioned, such as a weir, crashing waves or a babbling brook. Also, woodlands were considered to be treasured places. Broadleaved woodlands were generally preferred to be within, especially for relaxing and special moments, but

---

Box 5.1 Cultural ecosystem services of landscape (summarized from Natural England 2009a)

- Sense of history – a broad sense of the perceived permanence of nature and how humans have stood for centuries within it, and the continuity provided by places where people imagined many feet to have trod before. A sense of history was given by built historic features and remains, regardless of scale, ranging from major structures like castles to incidental ones like old stone stiles.
- Spiritual – a deep-seated, hard-to-access value, often delivered in more solitary moments. It could be delivered by iconic wildlife or a single tree, as well as by more traditional features such as burial mounds, standing stones, or churches. It was also associated with water (still lakes or slow-moving streams and rivers) and with high places, and could be created by the weather, such as a dramatic shaft of light or particular colours.
- Learning – many people, especially town dwellers, wanted their children to learn from being in a 'natural' landscape, for example going on nature trails or activity courses, and seeing animals and plants in their natural habitats. The achievement of climbing, or trekking a long distance, was an excellent way of learning about endurance and one's own capabilities.
- Leisure and activities – often linked to easily accessible places where there is a lot to do, such as municipal parks or the beach. Places that had rocks, crags or things to climb, as well as lanes and pathways, were also commonly identified. Features delivering this service were often either very dramatic, such as cliff faces, or very practical, such as a tea shop. They were often associated with an organized or group activity.
- Calm – often about intimate space, or moments of stillness that could be afforded by being in woods or just 'watching clouds'. It did not need dynamic or dramatic places, and simply the perception of remoteness could be important in delivering a sense of calm, as could the innocence of wildlife perceived in, for example, animals or carpets of snowdrops.
- A sense of place – any feature or landscape, and even certain wildlife species, could be considered to deliver a sense of place if they were local and distinctive to the area. People were proud of such places, because of their history or because they defined the mood of the local landscape. Areas that were disjointed or built-up were less successful in delivering this service.
- Inspiration – in order to produce this cultural benefit, the landscape had to be particularly beautiful, particularly dramatic, visceral, full of wildlife, romantic or powerful. It could also be very weather dependent.
- Escapism – this could be relatively easy to achieve, even in a very local landscape, although it generally required a feeling of remoteness, especially the absence of people. It was generally described in terms of contrast to stress and busy lives, and tended to be enhanced by certain sounds, and peacefulness.

coniferous woodlands were also valued for more active recreation. The enclosed atmosphere of woods was sometimes described as womb-like, and associated with childhood, achieving comforting and calming effects, although it could occasionally be frightening. For many people, the coast was an iconic place. Swimming and playing safely with families, of having fun, were important childhood memories; coast walks were important to many people at fundamental points in their lives, soul-searching by staring at the sea. Not surprisingly, mountains, hills and moors were often places of inspiration. Finally, certain landscape features – such as field systems, villages and lanes – seemed to anchor people's experience in history, enable them to learn about places, and contribute to a sense of wonderment at our role in the grand scheme of things.

A further basis for considering the way in which we connect with local, familiar landscapes is to draw upon the psychological concept of self-construct or sense of self. Cantrill and Senecah (2001) suggested that we partly construct our self-schema (Mandler, 1984) through our engagement with place. This influences how we make sense of the world around us, how we value it, and how we see other people who live in it and make claims over it. It suggests that there is a significant association between our sense of place, how the self gets related to the environment, and how we make sense of surroundings and events. Cantrill and Senecah (2001) argue that from the vantage of a 'sense of self-in-place', humans understand and process various claims and arguments regarding their relationship and responsibilities towards the natural world. It is also from this perspective that humans position themselves in relation to others advocating particular stances on alternative ways in which the landscape might be used. Thus, cognitive representations of the self-in-place form a link between how we interpret warnings about environmental change and how we actually behave or respond to development proposals. Our experiences regarding where we currently live, have resided in the past, or have visited colour the ways in which we view and communicate about the environment in general. In each of these places, there is a cultural world which is saturated with environmental references, and it is argued that we use these reference points to form distinct mental constructs – 'frames' – that affect the ways in which we acquire and process new information. Different frames result in different reactions to different environments, preferences for different types of activities, responses to environmental warnings and advice, and assumptions regarding one's vested self-interest in environmental issues. Especially for long-term residents, this sense of 'self-in-place' is strongly influenced by the residues of past relationships with humans, as well as with the land.

Taking a similar approach, Smith et al. (2011) looked at the relationship between place meanings and natural resource management, in rural areas where the natural resource base was central to people's surroundings and economy. Seven different aspects of place were considered – individual identity, family identity, self-efficacy, self-expression, community identity, economy and ecological integrity. These were statistically related to possible outcomes from resource management plans comprising ecological integrity, economy, lifestyle, quality of life, sense of space and social solidarity. The findings suggested that management objectives could play an important role in reinforcing the sense of 'physical space', particularly in relation to distinctive architecture, scenic attributes and urban scale. They could also enhance 'social solidarity' by fostering feelings of community and local pride.

A complementary approach is to draw upon sensemaking theory (Weick, 1995) as a way of understanding differences between the ways that people attend to or respond to their environment. Sensemaking is closely related to sense of identity, as people tend to make sense of the world in ways that are consistent with their sense of self, and in ways that make them feel good about themselves. We extract cues from the environment and then process them in order to create meaning, so that these cues become points of reference around which we develop a more general sense of what may be happening. The cues that each of us extracts from the environment depends on our psychological frame, as well as our identity, values, beliefs and past experiences – thus, meaning is constructed through a process of relating cues to frames, and cues are given meaning by relating them to past experiences, values and beliefs. Ford (2006) drew upon sensemaking theory in order to understand people's attitudes to clearfelling of forests in Tasmania. The values that we attach to the natural environment and our beliefs about the consequences of forest clearfelling are known to influence our judgements about the acceptability of different timber harvesting systems. The study showed how different groups of people, particularly local residents and tourists, attached different meanings to the same cues and so made different judgements about the acceptability of landscape management.

The term 'sense of place', although in widespread use, is often used in a rather vague way. Shamai and Ilatov (2005) have been amongst the most important contributors to a more rigorous and nuanced understanding of the term, and they have referred to two broad ways in which the term is applied by different researchers. In the first, sense of place or *genius loci* is used to explore several different aspects, notably topographical landscape features, built environment and people's own experiences. In the second, sense of place has been used to lay a greater emphasis on the way in which people experience, use and understand place, leading to a range of related notions such as place identity, place attachment, place dependency and insiderness. The authors note that the broad idea of sense of place has been explored by different disciplines drawing on very different theoretical and methodological traditions. For example humanist geography and social anthropology have been very influential in linking a sense of place with the idea of the rooted and healthy self, and have tended to focus on the insider's experience of buildings, streets or landscapes. This tends to allow people to describe the importance of place to them, rather than imposing policy-makers' terms, such as civic pride, on their experience. Environmental and social psychologists, by contrast, have mainly concentrated on turning these ideas into indicators that can be explored quantitatively. Key to these different perspectives is the relative importance of and interrelations between conscious and unconscious experience in understanding people's engagement with place.

On the one hand, therefore, some approaches have tended to use 'thick' descriptive qualitative methods to explore the complex nature of places in daily lived experience. Here, they try to understand individuals' behaviour by locating it within the wider contexts of their daily interactions by probing through field notes and in-depth interviews. This gives insight into how, through 'lived experience', people themselves draw together the different elements that make up place. Humanist geographers have looked at how people experience place in order to investigate phenomena such as 'placelessness' and the ways in which rootedness and people's attachments to place are being eroded. Using a phenomenological approach, geographers such as Relph (1976) and Tuan (1977) have emphasized how people inhabit place in a way that is not through conscious thought (cognition) but through their bodies, feelings and experiences.

On the other hand, social psychologists have studied 'place identity' as a complex cognitive structure, characterized by numerous attitudes, values, thoughts, beliefs, meanings and senses of belonging. Commonly, they have sought to measure these on a quantitative scale (e.g. Shamai and Kellerman, 1985). They see place identity as a cognitive substructure of self-identity, drawing upon a wide variety of cognitions related to the past, present and anticipated physical settings that define and circumscribe the day-to-day existence of a person (Proshansky et al., 1983). Thus, physical attributes of places have been identified as important influences on an individual's self-concept. Place identity has sometimes been elaborated into ideas of place attachment and place dependency, although there is little agreement on how these interrelate. For example, Jorgensen and Stedman (2006) have argued that a sense of place is best understood as being made up of place attachment (relating to an emotional engagement with place), place dependence (a conative property, directed towards action, and relying on the features of a place in order to do specific things), and place identity (which is mainly concerned with cognition and sensemaking).

Some authors have suggested that place attachment exists as a strong bond between people and places, in a way that develops over time. A qualitative study by Twigger-Ross and Uzzell (1996) identified three principles of place identity that allude to the ways in which place can build up individuals' positive state of mind, namely: distinctiveness, or the way people use place to distinguish themselves from others; continuity, where the idea of self is preserved over time, so that places allow a sense of continuity throughout the life course; and self-esteem, where place creates a positive evaluation of oneself. Unsurprisingly, place identity may emerge as a negative property in a grim and dispiriting landscape, possibly conferring a degree of stigmatization (Edelstein, 2004). Place attachment can form at a variety of geographic and spatial scales (Nanzer, 2004) from somewhere as local as the home or street,

---

Box 5.2 Links between social capital and sense of place (summarized from Graham et al., 2009)

- Place attachment and social networks seem to be linked in a virtuous cycle, although there is disagreement about which comes first and which is more important.
- Social networks may be more important than the built environment in generating place attachment, although certain types of built environment do provide safe and attractive public spaces that can support social activities and motivate people.
- A key way of understanding the relationship between sense of place and social capital is through the relationship between place attachment, self-esteem and shared pride.
- The more actively people are involved in heritage or place-shaping activities the greater the social capital developed.
- Social capital may also be linked to place dependency, as people meet others through shared interests and activities.
- The more actively that people are involved in place shaping, and the greater the opportunities for bridging and linking forms of social capital, then the greater becomes the likelihood of realizing social capital outcomes such as citizenship, well-being and the broadening of horizons.

---

to a country or even the whole planet. Place dependence, noted above, is also sometimes referred to as functional attachment and refers to the ways in which a place allows us to achieve our goals or carry out certain activities. Place dependence has been linked to place identity via the idea of self-efficacy (Korpela, 1989). Both place dependency and 'self-efficacy' tend to be used to describe the ways in which an individual will form stronger attachments to place when that place enables them to achieve their personal lifestyle goals.

Graham et al. (2009) looked more closely at the idea of 'sense of place' in relation to the historic landscape and specifically asked whether it is possible to identify relationships between the historic environment, sense of place and social capital (Box 5.2). This depends on linking place distinctiveness (what makes a place distinctive), place continuity (the way a place supports people's sense of continuity with others and with the past) and place dependency (how a place enables people to realize their goals). Links between social capital and sense of place can be traced in the relationship between place attachment and outcomes such as higher levels of self-esteem or pride in place. Further, heritage studies have explored the past as a means to support shared values and citizenship. One widely endorsed conclusion is that more active forms of engagement – creating, exhibiting and participating – have better outcomes in terms of generating social capital. It is also possible to see a link between place dependency and social capital through the kinds of social interactions that a place facilitates.

Arguments about the connections between people and landscape have tended to polarize between those researchers who think that people's identification with place is entirely a social construction, and those who believe that it relates to physical properties such as architectural character and distinctiveness. Research undertaken by Stedman and colleagues (Jorgensen and Stedman, 2001, 2006; Stedman, 2002, 2003) points to the likelihood that construction of place, and hence people's identification with particular landscapes, derives from a combination of both physical and social factors. Their studies have taken an integrated approach to characteristics of the environment, human uses of the environment, constructed meanings, and place attachment and satisfaction. For example, in one study of a lake-rich region in Wisconsin, they surveyed shoreline property owners, whose responses showed how certain physical landscape attributes, notably level of shoreline development, were strongly related to specific place attachment and satisfaction variables. Attitude theory – which draws together self-referent beliefs, emotions and behavioural commitments – was also used to explore complex relationships between the experience of a place and the particular landscape attributes of that place. Shoreline property owners were surveyed about their sense of place for their lakeshore properties. A predictive model comprising owners' age, length of ownership, participation in recreational activities, days spent on the property, extent of property development, and perceptions of environmental features, was employed to explain the variation in place identity, attachment and dependence. Perceptions of environmental features were found to be the biggest predictors of place dimensions. Matarrita-Cascante et al. (2010) similarly found a demonstrable effect of landscape-based factors (e.g. parks, forests, monuments, recreation areas) on people's community attachment. Whilst this was somewhat stronger for permanent residents, seasonal residents also displayed this to a significant degree.

Jorgensen and Stedman (2006) have drawn heavily on attitude theory as a way of explaining the sense of 'landscape place' in terms of cognitive (e.g. beliefs and perceptions), affective (e.g. emotions and feelings), and conative (e.g. behavioural intentions and commitments) domains. Attitude theory points to the distinctions between instrumental and consummatory behaviours: the former are driven by attitudes that have a strong cognitive basis and so are undertaken as a means to an end, whilst the latter are motivated by attitudes that are predominantly emotional (affect-based) and are performed for their own sake, enjoyment or interest. The differences between cognitive- and affect-based behaviours have consequences for attitude–behaviour relationships and attitude formation. Thus, sense of place can be conceived of as a multidimensional notion comprising place-specific beliefs (place identity), emotions (place attachment) and behavioural commitments (place dependence). Place identity therefore tends to represent beliefs that the self is defined in relation to a particular occupancy of landscape (in this instance, a lakeside property). Place attachment was defined in terms of positive feelings about this occupancy, while place dependence concerned the behavioural advantage of this particular occupancy relative to other settings (e.g. the extent to which a place facilitates certain types of recreation). Overall, sense of place seemed to be slightly more affect-based than either conative- or cognitive-based. As one confirmation of the ways in which physical landscape attributes contribute to place identity, for example, the most consistent predictor of sense of place proved to be property owners' attitudes to retaining native vegetation on their properties, with all three place dimensions being positively associated with this variable.

Other researchers give greater attention to the social construction of place (e.g. Manzo and Perkins, 2006). Castells (1983) has referred to space being 'produced' by factors that manifest themselves in everyday uses and meanings of place. Thus, who we are and where we feel we belong are influenced by aspects of our identity such as gender, race, ethnicity, socio-economic group, and whether we feel we are marginalized or whether we are an insider or outsider (Bradley et al., 2009). Such interactions can be traced in terms of conventional social-psychological factors. Thus, on the cognitive dimension, there is both place identity and community identity (i.e. one's sense of self as informed by neighbourhood places and by neighbourhood social interactions respectively). The affective dimension refers to one's emotional relationship to the neighbourhood or specific places within it and leads to place attachment, as well as one's emotional relationships with neighbours and other local community groups (sense of community). Finally, the behavioural dimension includes participation in community planning, preservation and development efforts (in regard to place-focused action) as well as engaging in neighbourly and other social activities (in regard to socially oriented behaviour). In particular, affective bonds to places can help inspire action because people are motivated to seek, stay in, protect and improve places that are meaningful to them. Thus, connections to place through social networks and other participatory and social learning processes complement those associated with physical attributes.

Age or position within the life course of an individual appears to influence sense of place, with younger individuals possibly attaching more importance to informal social groups and older ones to geographical places or the immediate home setting. Length of residence in a place has also been hypothesized as a potential predictor of place variables and, although the evidence is not entirely clear, it seems that individuals who have resided longer in a place are more likely to have developed significant relationships with other residents as well as with physical attributes of the place.

Eisenhauer et al. (2000) drew together the social and the physical by proposing that sense of place comprises two main components. First are the interactions among family or friends, family activities and traditions, and the memories associated with the people of the place. The second is based on a perception that the area possesses a natural uniqueness, associated with its scenery, climate, geology, environmental setting and wildlife. The natural and cultural environment, family and social activities, history and traditions are all important in the development of affective bonds with places (Kaltenborn and Williams, 2002). Broadly speaking, there appears to be a consensus amongst writers from several contrasting academic traditions that sense of place is a combination of both the physical–environmental and personal–social interaction in the place. However, location itself is not a sufficient condition to create a sense of, and attachment to, place: our conscious and subconscious association with a particular locality or region draws upon a long and deep experience of it, and the rituals, myths, meanings, symbols and qualities that we associate with it (Bradley et al., 2009).

Although it is widely alleged that quantity and quality of green space in an area will contribute positively to feelings about place, there are also significant concerns that green spaces can be associated with crime and antisocial activity, reducing people's feelings of safety, which in turn impacts negatively on quality of life. This feeling is often referred to as 'subjective social safety': people tend to behave, not on the basis of the actual riskiness of a place, but on how risky they perceive it to be. Thus, perceptions of social safety and perceived levels of crime, even though they are often unjustified, can have major implications for the image and use of a place. Certain environments may feel intrinsically safe or unsafe. On the one hand, green space is sometimes perceived as dangerous because it may facilitate crime by providing a hiding place for criminal activity; on the other, exposure to some types of natural environments appears to enhance feelings of social safety in a neighbourhood, because green space can reduce feelings of anger and aggression, as well as improve the level of informal surveillance (Kuo and Sullivan, 2001; Maas et al., 2009).

Maas et al. (2009) investigated whether the percentage of green space in people's living environment was associated with their subjective social safety. Specifically, they investigated the extent to which this relationship varies between urban and rural areas, between groups in the community that can be identified as more or less vulnerable, and between different types of green space. Based on a very large data set that linked people's feelings to the physical landscape of where they lived, the results suggested that higher levels of green space were associated with enhanced feelings of social safety, except in certain high-density urban areas. A possible explanation for the latter effect is that the scale and density of buildings in very strongly urban areas may affect fear of crime, and be poorly maintained. The study also found that women and elderly people feel safer in living environments with more green space, which would appear to contradict some other findings.

Olwig (2008) compares human attachment to place with the phenomenon of sheep hefting on or bonding themselves to various tracts of land. They become attached to particular grazing places through familiarity, so that the shepherd can expect them to follow a cyclical course as they move from meadow to meadow. The heft refers not only to the process by which sheep bond to the land but also to the social unit into which these sheep bond. In Scandinavian languages, animals 'heft' when they become accustomed to a new pasture, whilst people 'heft' as they become domiciled, settled or established in a place or occupation (Olwig, 2008). Whilst the application of animal behaviour to human meaning can only be metaphorical or figurative, it is extremely interesting that both derive from actual bodily engagement of walking the pasture. Where people continually walk and wear a path, and similarly make customary use of other elements of the environment, an area becomes woven together and shaped into what Olwig (1996) terms a 'substantive' landscape, created out of inhabitants' daily tasks and habits.

In central England, a project called the National Forest has sought, since the early 1990s, to transform a former coal mining landscape into a new landscape with a multifunctional potential and a new but distinctive character. There is now some evidence that people in the area are starting to develop a new sense of place (Morris and Urry, 2006). Researchers found that the Forest was positively perceived, especially because of improving environmental and economic conditions. These positive perceptions of place fed into a growing trust in and support for the institutional framework of the National Forest Company and its partner organizations, and of their vision. New social interactions were also emerging in people's experience of the Forest, with evident linkages between landscape change and a developing Forest 'sociality'. Forested places provided the setting for a reconfiguration of social networks and new forms of connectedness, including organized health walks (which have spin-offs in terms of new companionships), and volunteering undertaken by local companies through corporate social responsibility programmes. Other volunteer activities and 'friends of' groups have emerged, whilst an increase in physical access has led to a significant transformation of the relationship between farmers and the wider community. Both physical and 'mental' access are leading to stronger relationships between people and the Forest itself, both as they adapt to it as 'their area' and engage in acts of remembering the area's industrial past and of imagining its future. In relation to the area's changing economy, the Forest is acting as a catalyst for new networks of cooperation between economic and political actors.

Health and well-being

As noted previously, landscape appears significantly to influence our physical and mental health, and more general well-being. Studies in some developed countries suggest that well under half of their population is sufficiently physically active to meet the recommended minimum of 30 minutes of moderate activity five times a week, and there are major concerns about increasing levels of obesity and their associated health service costs. Regular physical activity contributes to the prevention of more than twenty health conditions, so that people who are physically active reduce their risk of developing major chronic diseases such as heart disease, stroke, some cancers and type II diabetes (Chartered Institution of Water and Environmental Management, 2010).

Ward Thompson (2011) traced the connections between the landscape and people's health, from ancient times to the present day, noting how access to nature and attractive green spaces has been a recurrent theme in descriptions of therapeutic environments and associated healthy lifestyles. She describes how the theme of health in the picturesque debates of eighteenth century England (including such concepts as 'active curiosity') was taken up and developed in arguments for the nineteenth century urban park movement in England and North America. Latterly, the links between health, nature and access have been explored scientifically and related to modern urban lifestyles. However, although the salutogenic value of landscapes has been long recognized, researchers are still barely beginning to understand the causal mechanisms between landscape and health.

Research projects tend either to look at the psychological, restorative benefits of visual contact with vegetation and other nature, or the physiological dimensions of stress and restoration. For example, Ulrich (1981, 1984, 1992, 1999) used a range of empirical evidence to argue that the benefits of viewing green space or other nature goes beyond aesthetic enjoyment to include enhanced emotional well-being, reduced stress and, in certain situations, improved health. Other studies found that prison inmates used health-care facilities significantly less often if the view from their cells was toward natural areas (Kaplan, 1992).

In terms of physical health, the landscape provides opportunities for exercise as well as more wholesome air and water, and possibly quicker recovery from certain medical procedures. In terms of mental health, it contributes to tranquillity, relaxation, restoration and companionship. In terms of wider well-being, it can promote more positive mood and stronger self-identity. In practice, field-based evidence does not clearly distinguish between these different aspects, and in terms of the human experience they often overlap and are not easily compartmentalized for analysis. Many of the illustrations in this section have implications, therefore, for several aspects of human health and well-being at once.

One study (Fuller et al., 2007) entailed undertaking surveys in a range of urban and suburban green spaces in Sheffield, and found that users were able to detect the degree of biodiversity on a site and that, as biodiversity increased, so did their level of psychological benefit. The researchers used various measures related to well-being – such as reflection, distinctive identity, continuity with the past and attachment – and found that these were positively associated with measures such as plant richness, bird richness and number of habitat types. People proved to be quite good at estimating levels of biodiversity in green spaces, especially in relation to the more visible and static components of biodiversity such as variety of plant species and habitat type. The increase in psychological well-being with species richness and the accurate assessment of richness levels were surmised to operate through some proxy mechanism – most probably, overall habitat structure and variety act as cues to the perceptions and benefits of biodiversity. If this is the case, management emphasizing a mosaic of habitat patches may enhance the well-being of urban people, as well as biodiversity levels and ecosystem service provision. The results indicate that simply providing green space overlooks the fact that spaces can vary dramatically in their contribution to human health and biodiversity provision, and so it would be a good idea for green space managers to aim to increase, as well as conserve, biodiversity.

Numerous studies have documented that experiences in, or of, nature can be beneficial for human health and well-being, and these have been systematically reviewed by Morris (2003). Morris notes how even relatively brief contact with nature has been reported to have psychological benefits by reducing stress, improving attention, having a positive effect on mental restoration, and moderating attention deficits. In addition to mental advantages, there appear to be direct physical health benefits, such as increased longevity, recovery from surgery and self-reported health. The availability of nature correlates positively with health: benefits have been associated with various types of nature experiences including wilderness, neighbourhood parks, gardens and natural features around residences. The stress reducing effect of nature may be a key element as stress plays a role in the aetiology and course of several common health problems, including cardiovascular diseases, anxiety disorders and depression. A main concern with most of the studies mentioned above is to decipher what is actually causing the benefits. Ulrich points to four possible advantages: being in nature tends to correlate with physical activity, which obviously promotes health; nature activities often imply socializing, for example walking together or sitting in a park with friends, and building social networks; nature offers temporary escape from everyday routines and demands; and it is possible that the interaction with nature itself has an appreciable impact on the mind, so that there may be a specific benefit from learning and performing tasks in a natural environment. The idea that being in nature may improve health has led to organized activities such as therapeutic horticulture, where a group of people comes together to do gardening and similar tasks. Therapeutic horticultural activities have apparently had some success, primarily for people with mental health problems or learning difficulties, although empirical evidence is limited.

There are at least three possibilities why nature itself may bring these benefits: the air may be healthier in that it contains fewer pollutants and higher humidity; the plants may emit fragrances that humans find pleasant or react to in various ways; and the visual experience of plants may make a difference. It appears that whilst viewing images of nature may have some beneficial effect, the direct view or experience of 'real' nature has an appreciable additional effect. It has been reported that viewing natural landscapes provides psychological and health benefits, including a reduction in stress, mental restoration, and improved mood simply by being consciously or unconsciously pleasing to the eye. Ulrich (1984), in a renowned but much debated paper, used medical records to infer that a hospital window with a view of nature would improve healing, reflected in a reduced level of pain medication and quicker recovery after surgery. Natural landscapes have a consistent positive health effect, while urban landscapes can have a negative effect (Velarde et al., 2007). Kaplan and Kaplan (1989) point out that distant nature or wilderness are not the only settings conducive to restorative experiences, and that small, nearby nature possesses the crucial benefit of proximity.

Place identity may also have restorative benefits. Thus, Korpela (1991) has suggested that restorative experiences figure in emotional- and self-regulation processes through which individuals develop place identity: people often go to their favourite places to relax, calm down and clear their minds after threatening or emotionally negative events (Korpela, 1989; Korpela and Hartig, 1996). Indeed, familiarity with and direct experience and knowledge of a place will affect preference for it (Livingston et al., 2008). Environmental self-regulation in this way appears to provide a clear link between restorative environments and the concept of place identity. Favourite places are generally places with greenery, water, and scenic quality. Here, restoration occurs, firstly, because of increased physical activity and its attendant benefits of enhanced mood, reduced stress and more positive self-concept and, secondly, because of the sensory qualities of the surroundings. The literature suggests that there are five key ways in which exposure to the natural environment is beneficial in this regard: enhanced personal and social communication skills; increased physical health; enhanced mental and spiritual health; enhanced spiritual, sensory and aesthetic awareness; and ability to assert personal control, possibly through an increased sensitivity to one's own well-being (Morris, 2003).

There are two broad ways in which landscape can contribute to physical health: by encouraging people to take more exercise; and by generally improving the liveability and salubriousness of areas. In terms of exercise, the most obvious opportunity is that of walking, which, in developed countries, is now typically a form of recreation rather than a major mode of transport. Brisk walking is a simple and effective way of developing and maintaining cardiorespiratory fitness, body composition, muscular strength and endurance in adults. Walking can also restore natural perception and reconnect human beings with the physical world of nature (Edensor, 2000). Thus, doctors will now often prescribe 'health walks' and organized participation in gardening and wildlife conservation tasks ('green gyms'). Outdoor activity is widely thought to provide an escape from the pressures of modern living, achieve an enhanced state of relaxation and refreshment, tackle new challenges, and help reduce anxiety and stress levels. Participants, in particular those with depression, in Green Gym projects have also noted improved mental health and enhanced feelings of well-being as a result of taking part (BTCV, 2002). Further, there may be an enhanced spiritual, sensory and aesthetic awareness associated with feeling the wind and sun, hearing water, smelling vegetation and so forth. Outdoor recreation and, in particular, walking is a multi-sensory and stimulating experience that frees the mind and generates reflexivity, philosophical and intellectual thought, aesthetic contemplation and opens up a more 'natural' self (Edensor, 2000). Health Walk and Green Gym participants have reported that, in addition to health benefits, they also experience a sense of regaining a 'contact with nature' (Bird, 2007).

Activity in the landscape is also beneficial to personal and social communication skills. Participation in activities within natural open spaces can help build confidence and self-esteem, develop basic social skills, and maintain or improve quality of life, as well as providing participants with a new topic of conversation (Morris, 2003). Milligan and Bingley (2007) identified benefits for young adult mental health service users in undertaking activities in woodland environments, and related this partly to the sense of achievement in completing skills-based tasks. Roe and Aspinall (2011) have similarly found that affordances provided in a forest landscape had a beneficial effect on boys with extreme behavioural problems. They reported positive changes in affective responses over time, associated with increased trust, exploratory activity and social cohesion. It appeared that there was evidence not only of short-term 'restoration', but also of longer term 'instoration' (Hartig et al., 1996) of well-being.

At a more general level, Kahn and Kellert (2002) have assembled extensive evidence on the need for children to have rich contact with nature for their physical, emotional, intellectual and even moral development. In this context, Louv (2005) has identified the condition of 'nature-deficit disorder', which he argues arises from children's progressive loss of contact with nature. This phenomenon, resulting from the increasingly indoor and virtual nature of children's leisure, and even educational, time is proposed as a major contributor to trends such as rises in obesity, attention disorders and depression. Louv argues that society is teaching young people to avoid direct experience in nature, partly as a result of over-regulation of outdoor pursuits and partly due to the demotion of traditional disciplines such as zoology and geology in favour of more remunerative and patentable subjects. Hence, as young people spend less and less of their lives in natural surroundings, their richness of experience is diminished. Louv argues that this trend runs counter to emerging evidence about the links between contact with nature and our mental, physical and spiritual health. Indeed, it is noted that increasing the exposure of youngsters to nature in specific ways is becoming an acknowledged mode of therapy for attention-deficit disorders and other maladies. Reducing the 'nature deficit' of young people would appear to be important both for their well-being and for the future of the planet. One specific educational opportunity afforded by green space is the Forest School, which originated in Europe in the early twentieth century as a way of teaching about the natural world, and latterly has been formalized into some educational programmes. The 'school' involves participants journeying, preferably by foot, to a local woodland environment to learn outdoors on a regular sustained basis, and it has been found to support social, emotional and physical development. The 'school' may be used simply to develop awareness and competencies or, more formally, as a setting for the delivery of vocational training in rural skills (http://www.foresteducation.org/).

There is varied evidence on the value of wilderness experiences and outward bound courses as effective forms of complementary therapy, typically for patients with mental health illness, adolescents with challenging behaviour, post-traumatic stress disorder war veterans, and people who abuse alcohol and drugs. For example, Haugan et al. (2006) have demonstrated the therapeutic benefits of landscape through the Green Care programme in Norway, which offers farm-based services to schools and to health and social care services. Here, farms host a wide range of activities, such as kindergartens, after-school programmes, day care, school projects and theme assignments, education adapted to pupils with special needs, and activities and tasks designed for psychiatric patients, mentally impaired adults and dementia sufferers. Useful activities are undertaken in a stress-free environment, focusing on learning via practical challenges and experiences, together with social training and interaction. Similar benefits have also widely been associated with purpose-designed, healing gardens, and 'therapeutic horticulture' has sometimes been practised as a way of involving users directly in the maintenance of such spaces (Beckwith and Gilster, 1997; Cooper-Marcus and Barnes, 1999).

Pauleit et al. (2003) have drawn attention to the design implications of encouraging greater public engagement in green space. First, the size of areas is important – for example, parks develop an interior climate when they are larger than 1 hectare, whilst research into woodland recreation indicates an area of 2 hectares as the smallest wood that people wish to visit regularly. Second, accessibility matters, as the vast majority of park users reach a park on foot. A walk of approximately 5–6 minutes length from home seems to be a threshold beyond which the frequency of green space use sharply declines. Third, perceived naturalness of green space is important. However, whilst ecologists value areas in terms of species richness and occurrence of rare species, most green space users perceive 'naturalness' more often as a tranquil contrast to urban life and activities. The experience of nature is an important quality a park should offer to be attractive, but it is rarely the predominant one. Finally, connection of green spaces into wider systems is also beneficial to users, for example by moderating air temperatures in surrounding built areas, and providing useful walking and cycling routes.

Considering the wider health benefits of salubrious places (though this will also to some extent reflect increased levels of physical activity) some compelling evidence has been presented by Mitchell and Popham (2009). This study examined large national data sets on general mortality, cause-specific mortality, income and green space, and the connections between them. The authors postulated that income-related inequality in health would be less pronounced in populations with greater exposure to green space, since access to such areas can modify the disease pathways that tend to be associated with low socio-economic position. In relation to low income groups, the evidence revealed significant differences between categories of exposure to green space in relation to mortality from all causes and, more specifically, from circulatory disease. Health inequalities that tend to be related to income deprivation were similarly lower in populations living in the greenest areas. By contrast, causes of death that were unlikely to be affected by landscape, such as lung cancer and intentional self-harm, showed no difference between areas with different levels of green space. The evidence strongly suggested that populations that have access to the greenest environments have the lowest levels of health inequality: improving physical environments by adding green space of sufficient quality and quantity in areas of income deprivation and low socio-economic status might therefore reduce socio-economic health inequalities. The broader health-related contributions of green space are primarily associated with air quality. For example, high traffic densities in urban areas can result in pollutants exceeding European Union targets for nitrogen dioxide (NO_2) and particulate matter of ten micrometers or less (PM_{10}), with NO_2 particularly linked to asthma. Green infrastructure can help to ameliorate air pollution and, through providing more attractive green transport solutions, reduce the reliance on cars for short journeys (Chartered Institution of Water and Environmental Management, 2010).

Linking active transport networks

Sustainable transport strategies aim to reduce the carbon footprint associated with human movement patterns. They do this in various ways, which also aim to have a number of spin-offs such as raising fitness levels by encouraging 'active transport' (i.e. travel that requires physical work, such as walking or cycling). Key ways in which this can be achieved are by installing a convenient and safe network of footpaths and cycle routes, encouraging the use of smaller or alternative-fuel cars, reducing the impact of motor traffic by promoting 'shared space' of streets, making public transport more attractive, and reducing the distances that people have to travel to work or school. Clearly, the urban landscape is an important contributor to these activities, especially by affording a connective infrastructure for active transport. UK government policy has sought to use the planning process to make cycling, walking and public transport the modes of choice, so that these modes become more convenient for the majority of journeys than car usage (Department for Transport, 2008). This aim, however, was made in the context of growth points and ecotowns where infrastructure can often be planned rationally from the outset; the normal situation, by contrast, is usually one of having to reconnect routeways by retrofitting them into inherited urban structures, which is much more difficult.

The Greenways concept, pioneered in the USA, implies corridors of protected public and private lands that link recreational, cultural and natural features and provide multiple public benefits. Often, the most practical way of creating greenways is to base them on rivers, stream valleys, mountain ridges, abandoned railroad corridors, utility wayleaves, canals, scenic roads and other linear features (Ahern, 1995). Turner (1995) proposed a simple but effective definition of a greenway as 'a route which is good from an environmental point of view'; he also suggested a more eloquent one, namely, 'a linear space containing elements planned, designed and managed for multiple purposes including ecological, recreational, cultural, aesthetic and other purposes compatible with the concept of sustainable land use' (Turner, 2006). Five key ideas are associated with greenways – a linear configuration, linkage, multifunctionality, consistency with sustainability, and integration (Ahern, 1995). The rural Greenways and Quiet Lanes programme piloted in England between 1998 and 2002 tested the concept of a largely off-road network – often drawing upon existing routes such as cycle trails and canal towpaths – to connect people to facilities and open spaces in and around towns, cities and the countryside. Although substantial lengths of greenway were created, in practice they were found to lack a coherent network, with many routes suffering from some form of severance that made journeys on them unattractive or impossible. Also, they tended to link very few useful origins and destinations in relation to the majority of 'trip generators' (e.g. offices, factories, schools).

Official guidance indicates that a network planning approach should be adopted for potential new routes, based on sound research into the nature of demand, and drawing upon existing routes for walking, cycling and horse riding. One of the benefits of greenway planning is to plan and manage these networks in an integrated way that reflects users' experience, realizing opportunities for different users to share routes whilst at the same time being aware of points of incompatibility. Practice, though, often falls short of policy. One survey in the UK found that greenway planning lacked enthusiasm and direction; most greenways were in practice just linear public open spaces with a trail path rather than multi-objective landscapes, and they were usually designed by generalists rather than staff with specialist knowledge of green space planning (Turner, 2006). Although extensive experience has now been gained, difficulties persist. The Glasgow and Clyde Valley Green Network in Scotland provides an excellent example of a partnership approach, supported by national policy commitments and a city–region landscape framework. Even so, significant barriers to implementation have been encountered, such as lack of linkages to adjacent green space, limited quality of local green space, and shortcomings in path networks, cycling facilities and public transport (Smith et al., 2008; Chartered Institution of Water and Environmental Management, 2010).

Whilst most experience has been gained in rural areas, the problems of route fragmentation and retrofitting networks into intensive land uses are greatly compounded in urban areas. The European Greenways Association, for example, as well as promoting rural recreational routes, has emphasized the urban case for inserting dedicated active-transport routes adjacent to motorized traffic routes and restoring decommissioned former transport routes to create additional links. Many cities in North America are attempting to implement connected greenway networks and, whilst some have only a sparse existing open space resource from which to develop a network, others have inherited an impressive historic open space framework. Erickson (2004) investigated practice in Milwaukee (USA) and Ottawa (Canada) and considered the current situation in relation to open space planning and greenway development, as well as the performance of local planning structures and leadership. Both cities had a substantial framework for greenway development resulting from their historic development, notably the riverside parkways planned in the early twentieth century. However, regional greenways planning had been piecemeal, and lacked proper coordination and vision. More optimistically, both cities had incipient integrated greenways programmes, with some innovative experimental projects and growing institutional capacity. Neither city had a coordinated greenways plan in place, a broad vision that could be mapped, nor an agency with the authority to implement it; yet some agencies had concern for greenway objectives and were collaborating in targeted, opportunistic areas.

A noted success story in linear green infrastructure running right through a large city and providing multiple benefits has been the Chattanooga and Hamilton County Greenway in Tennessee, USA (Forest Research, 2010). The first section of the greenway, the Tennessee River Park, was created in the late 1980s and the Greenway Advisory Board was convened by the City of Chattanooga authorities in 1989, largely formed from grass roots organizations seeking a high quality greenway along the waterfronts and scenic corridors that connected housing, parks, businesses and tourist attractions. The authorities proposed a 16 kilometre park along each side of the Tennessee River, comprising large hubs that anchor a system of links and smaller sites made up of natural, historical, cultural and recreational features. To assist in the planning and implementation, the city contracted with the Trust for Public Land (a non-profit organization) to provide technical assistance, coordination, land purchase and land protection, so that a key feature of the Chattanooga greenways networks is that the main coordinating body is citizen-led. The greenways are progressively being networked into a linear park largely based on donated land and easements, reserved for environmental and recreational use. The Florida greenways programme (Conservation Fund, 2004) further illustrates the need to base planning and action on a broadly based group of stakeholders and mixed funding sources, coordinated by an organization with appropriate gravitas (in this case, the Florida Greenways Commission). It demonstrates the need to avoid a purely opportunistic approach that creates 'connections for connection's sake', or a join-the-dots approach. It has also been claimed that the network helps to connect residents and visitors to the state's natural heritage, enhance their sense of place and enrich their quality of life.

Urban food production

Urban agriculture is agriculture that occurs within the city. Occasionally this may include small animals and aquaculture, but in most cases concentrates on high yield gardening for fruit and vegetable growing (Viljoen et al., 2005). It sometimes utilizes vertical and horizontal intensification of land use, increasing the number of activities on a particular piece of land by overlaying one use above the other, planting on fences and walls, and multi-cropping. Peri-urban agriculture is agriculture occurring in the urban–rural fringe, or within peripheral low-density suburban areas, and tends to occupy larger sites. Cities and their immediate surroundings thus have an 'urban productive area'. This UPA is generally characterized by the production of seasonal and local food, often organically produced.

In various countries there are already long-standing examples of an effective UPA. For example, in the UK there has been a long tradition of allotments – small non-commercial plots clustered together in groups and leased to individuals by local authorities. These experienced a serious decline in condition and interest during the mid-twentieth century but latterly have recovered strongly. Reflecting a widespread continental European tradition, Germany's *schrebergärten* are similar to allotments but are typically used as weekend leisure gardens, often with a small summer house, as well as for food production. In Cuba, *parcelas* and *huertos intensivos* are like large allotments farmed by a family or group of individuals, whilst *organiponicos* are high-yield urban commercial market gardens producing food for sale to the public based on the Chinese bio-intensive model of raised beds and intensive organic farming methods. Community gardens, managed and used by local communities or neighbourhoods for recreation and education, have been widely established on unused or abandoned urban sites, or in the grounds of public buildings such as hospitals and retirement homes. City farms and urban farms are similar to a community garden, but with some poultry and small animals. Their significance is educational rather than productive, although a limited quantity of produce may be generated. In addition, the gardens of homes are widely used for fruit and vegetable growing (Viljoen et al., 2005; Mougeot, 2006).

Urban agriculture has been championed as a way of reconnecting communities with their productive landscape. It is likely to increase food security, namely, giving populations both economic and physical access to a supply of food, sufficient in both quality and quantity, at all times, regardless of climate and harvest, social level and income (Petts, 2001). In addition, it may also increase 'fungible income', namely, the indirect income gained from the substitution of market-bought produce. Modes of production are often labour intensive, involving local people and being much less reliant on mechanization and chemical inputs than mainstream agriculture. Modes of marketing typically entail food being directly consumed by the producers or marketed through a range of local outlets, thereby minimizing 'food miles'. More broadly, urban agriculture has benefits in terms of healthy diet, and community organization and cohesion. Arguably, urban and urban fringe agriculture can, by stimulating the whole of the food supply chain, contribute to job opportunities, reduction of urban poverty, community engagement, reduced energy costs, smarter use of resources such as recycled water and organic waste, and improved nutrition.

It has been reported (Commission for Architecture and the Built Environment, n.d.) that food production, processing and transportation is responsible for 8 per cent of the average person's total carbon footprint and 23 per cent of their ecological footprint. Garnett (2000) had previously shown how London's food system exemplifies and symbolizes its fundamental unsustainability. The city's ecological footprint is 125 times its surface area, requiring the equivalent of the entire productive area of Britain to sustain itself. Although local authority recycling and composting schemes have led to some improvement, London was at the time of the study creating nearly 900,000t of organic waste a year, of which households contributed over 600,000t (40 per cent of total domestic waste). It has been suggested that our food-related footprint could be reduced by using green space in towns and cities to grow food in community orchards, market gardens, allotments and school grounds, as well as in private gardens. A number of initiatives were established around the UK in the early twenty-first century such as the Manchester Joint Health Unit food strategy to bring some food production and composting activities within the city, creating a more closed loop system; Incredible Edible Todmorden, aiming to achieve local self-sufficiency in vegetables, for example by replacing some ornamental planting in local parks, planters and flower beds with vegetables, herbs and fruit; Capital Growth (London), supporting communities wanting to grow their own food, for example by facilitating access to land, and running an Edible Estates competition to reward community food projects; Middlesbrough's

Urban Farming project, which included a 'town meal' as the focal point for an annual programme of growing and harvesting, and 'grow-zones' on public land; and the Offshoots permaculture project in Burnley whose role extended into horticulture, social work, therapy and food production, as well as community schemes such as composting.

Ravenscroft and Taylor (2009) reviewed the phenomenon of food citizenship as a result of people participating consciously within a localized food system. Such activity helps to develop various competencies – analytical competencies (making connections), relational competencies (new forms of organizational relationships between actors in the food chain), ethical competencies (valuing of non-market goods), aesthetic and spiritual competencies (connecting agriculture and food with beauty), and physical (exercise and skills-related) competency. Many of the benefits of localized food systems are associated with shortening the food chain so that citizens gain better knowledge of both the production processes and the actual producer of the food. At the heart of this new relationship is the generation of a new way of living with, as opposed to from, the land. Thus, reducing the spatial and cultural distance between producer and consumer may well result in urban communities becoming more responsible for the food they eat and for land care. However, Ravenscroft and Taylor argue that if we simply see this as an alternative method of producing food, we may lose sight of the deeper bonds between localization and sustainability associated with community action (civil labour). Urban food production may thus be viewed as a type of regenerative agriculture, which incorporates a community of people engaged in civil labour to produce food and its associated landscape. Common forms of regenerative agricultural enterprise include community 'share' farming, community-owned social enterprise, and various forms of land trust.

Viljoen et al. (2005) have promoted the idea of a spatially connected UPA that they describe as a continuous productive urban landscape (CPUL). This is a design concept that advocates the coherent introduction of interlinked productive landscapes into cities as an essential element of sustainable urban infrastructure. Central to the CPUL concept is the creation of multifunctional open urban space networks that complement and support the built environment. Key features of CPUL space include urban agriculture, leisure and commercial outdoor spaces, natural habitats, ecological corridors and circulation routes for non-vehicular traffic. Its network connects existing open urban spaces, maintaining and, in some cases, modifying their current uses. Within the CPUL concept, urban agriculture refers in the main to fruit and vegetable production, as this provides the highest yields per square metre of urban ground. Typical urban agriculture practices range from small-scale food gardening to high yield, space-efficient market gardening.

Lovell (2010), in a US context, has argued that urban agriculture offers an alternative land use for integrating multiple functions in densely populated areas. While urban agriculture has historically been an important element of cities in many developing countries, recent concerns about economic and food security have resulted in a growing movement to produce food in cities of developed countries. In these regions, urban agriculture offers a new frontier for land use planners and landscape architects to become involved in the development and transformation of cities to support community farms, allotment gardens, rooftop gardening, edible landscaping, urban forests and other productive features of the urban environment. Despite the growing interest in urban agriculture, urban planners and landscape architects are often ill-equipped to integrate food-systems thinking into future plans for cities. The challenge is to design urban agriculture spaces to be multifunctional, matching the specific needs and preferences of local residents, while also protecting the environment (Table 5.1).

Connecting economy to landscape

Earlier, we noted the operation of virtuous and vicious circles in the development of cultural landscapes. However, linking mainstream economy to the direct production of valued landscape, as has formerly happened serendipitously in certain times and places, is not well charted. In essence, the linkage of landscape to economy in complex modern society is hardly ever wholly spontaneous because of the ubiquity of the influence of the state and transnational markets and cultures. The state intervenes to control the nature of built development including, in some countries, the subdivision of land; it grant-aids and directly undertakes the regeneration of damaged or impoverished landscapes; and it supports the continuation of landscapes that deliver multiple ecosystem services. Private sector effects are also highly diffuse and transnational, with outside investors and agribusiness operators impacting on local landscapes. Nevertheless, it is possible to couple market-based processes to landscape production, in two main ways.

First, certain economic outputs may directly draw upon landscape qualities in their production and marketing. The most obvious ones are tourism (especially 'green' tourism) and niche agriculture. Green tourism (Fennell, 2008) may directly generate expenditure and employment linked to specific qualities of local environments, and it may also recover funds from tourists through 'visitor payback' schemes (Scott et al., 2003). Speciality foods often benefit from their 'typicity' and thus can command a premium based on the landscape reputation of their areas of origin. One study in England (Land Use Consultants, 2006) identified over one hundred locality foods with a clear link to specific landscapes that, through their production methods and/or links to semi-natural habitats, brought clear landscape benefits. The researchers considered that this number was likely to be a significant underestimate of the total number of such foods. An interesting case of the operation of a virtuous circle has been demonstrated by Wood et al. (2007) who found that grazing animals on biodiverse pastures produced meat with

Table 5.1 Planning measures that can support the multifunctional benefits of urban agriculture (summarized from Lovell, 2010)

Function	Issues	Possible planning measures
Production	Capable of yielding fruits, vegetables, fungi, herbs, medicinal plants, meats, dairy and other products.	Provide suitable, accessible, and safe land with good solar access and water availability.
Energy conservation	Localized production reduces the embodied energy associated with inputs, transport and packaging.	Develop supportive local transport networks.
Waste management	Organic waste products can be composted and used as fertilisers for urban agriculture and horticulture.	Improve municipal waste management to optimize recycling of organic wastes.
Biodiversity	Urban agriculture can support a wide range of species, and help retain traditional cultivars.	Convert some open space areas of low diversity (e.g. turf) to community gardens and farms.
Microclimate control	Beneficial effects on microclimate through humidity control, wind alleviation, greening and shade.	Promote edible plantings in built-up areas to combat the heat island effect and other unfavourable climatic conditions.
Urban greening	Community and domestic farming contribute to the greening of urban areas, improving aesthetics and well-being.	Support efforts to convert vacant and derelict land into productive green spaces for use by residents.
Economic revitalization	Cooperative and social enterprises can create new jobs for neighbourhood residents and support local economies.	Create networks to connect workers, farmers and markets to help retain and grow new ventures.
Community socialization	Gardening and farming can promote social interaction through sharing food, knowledge and labour.	Along with community gardens, integrate other activities and features to encourage socializing.
Human health	Urban agriculture offers healthy food and encourages physical activity, as well as improving green space access generally.	Involve medical practices etc in promoting gardening/farming as a healthy lifestyle.
Cultural heritage	Urban agriculture can provide access to ethnic foods that are typically not available in existing markets.	Integrate community garden spaces into culturally diverse areas.
Education	Children and adults learn about foods, nutrition, cooking, environment, economics and cultures through urban agriculture.	Integrate gardening and urban agriculture into curricula and other programmes.

improved taste and distinctiveness. Thus, farmers were incentivized to invest in the landscape because their output could demand a market premium.

The second way is by the potential of attractive landscape to attract and retain inward investment. Although there has been some apparently conflictual evidence regarding the likelihood of landscape being a significant attractor of new investors, there is stronger evidence that entrepreneurs are reluctant to leave areas of fine landscape (Johnson and Rasker, 1995) and that the presence of green space impacts positively on land values (Nicholls and Crompton, 2005). In practice, some of the most extensive 'landscaping', i.e. deliberate establishment of new amenity planting, has been associated with the development of industrial and business areas and their associated access networks. The 'Creating a Setting for Investment' project in South Yorkshire (Henneberry et al., 2004; Rowley et al., 2008) looked specifically at the role of landscape in modern business investment, which is extremely difficult though very important to ascertain. There appeared to be considerable differences between the views of land valuation professionals (who tend to use rather conservative investment criteria), those who speculated in land investment (often very distanced from the daily occupants of the land), and those who actually worked on the sites. Broadly, valuers expressed the view that the landscape quality of a site and its immediate setting would have a moderate impact on land values, and there was wider evidence that varying the landscape quality of the setting could have an impact on the image of the site and area, confidence in the area and the quality of the site as a business location. In the study, the locations where these factors rated more highly – the higher quality settings – attracted on average higher rents and were easier to let. There was stronger evidence that the occupants of business premises attached higher importance to landscape quality than did distant investors, possibly resulting in higher workforce satisfaction, performance and retention. In this context, positive landscape features included being visually attractive, having a 'cared for' appearance in both design and maintenance, having useful facilities and being pleasant to use.

Conclusion

Despite the criticisms levelled by many academics at the notion of local connections between people and place, it remains popular with policy makers. Our cultures and connections may be increasingly virtual and global, but the idea of physical and psychological associations with nearby landscapes remains intuitively compelling. Politicians and planners still promote the case for engaging communities in their local landscapes, in the belief that this will both intensify a 'sense of place' and pride in place.

There is considerable evidence that, whilst place-ness may in some degree be a social construction, it is also anchored in physical landscape properties (Figure 5.2). There is also extensive evidence that the local landscape

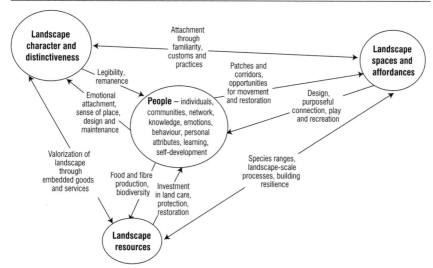

Figure 5.2 A summary of linkages between people and their landscapes

significantly affects our physical and mental well-being. Loss of connections with local landscape may contribute to declining fitness and health, whilst immersing particular groups of people in the landscape may provide them with a restorative 'dose' of natural treatment.

In addition to social and psychological benefits, the landscape may also provide economic ones. It would seem that embedding economic activities in the landscape can create new opportunities and generate higher returns. Planners and entrepreneurs may therefore feel motivated to invest in landscape improvements as a way of generating or retaining inward investment, and developing new landscape-related goods and services.

Improving the connectedness of urban landscapes can create opportunities for food production and active transport. As well as contributing to improved health and fitness, the promotion of reconnected landscapes close to where people live can also increase our capacity to adapt and respond to environmental change. The local landscape itself provides a vivid setting for social learning about real and tangible issues. It creates a forum in which future options for living with nature, for example in relation to flooding or urban climatic comfort, can be explored by different stakeholders (Selman et al., 2010). It will also tend to increase security against future 'shocks', for example by reducing our reliance on carbon-based transport or on imported food.

Achieving landscape reconnection thus involves equal consideration of the physical and the social. It may, however, involve controversial measures, or the acceptance of landscape changes that conflict with our innately conservative attitudes towards scenic aesthetics. The final chapter looks at some of the conceptual and practical ways of addressing these issues.

Chapter 6

Landscape connectivity in the future

Thinking and doing

Introduction

This book broadly assumes that enhanced connectivity of landscape will tend to increase future multifunctionality, sustainability and resilience. This final chapter considers two broad areas where human action needs to be directed for this to occur. First is the ethical and conceptual basis for the ways in which we relate to the wider landscape, and to its usage by many communities of interest. Second is the broad sphere of policy and practice, where governance and stakeholder actions need to be increasingly joined-up in order to address complex and uncertain future problems.

Thinking about landscape connectivity

Landscape has often been appraised in terms of aesthetics – the different types of beauty that different people see in it. This varies enormously, from people who seek a very artistic and formal elegance in designed landscape to those who seek a sublime experience of wilderness, from those who seek out special and dramatic scenery to those who value the familiarity of everyday spaces, and from those who seek out unspoilt countryside to those who enjoy the landscape of enterprise and productivity. Sometimes we may value different things simultaneously. As an added complication, our aesthetic appreciation of landscape is not static. Aesthetics seem to be partly innate, as humans are programmed to find satisfaction in certain types of complex visual patterning, and partly acquired, according to changing social norms and narratives. As an illustration of an 'acquired' aesthetic, we might, for example, begin by perceiving wind turbines as an intrusive blot on a landscape, but, if we become persuaded by the case for locally produced renewable energy, start to see them as a symbol of harmony between people and nature. We might start by seeing naturalistic ecological planting designs as scruffy and weed-infested but, as we gain insight into the nature of urban ecosystems, begin to prefer them to manicured gardenesque planting with non-native species. Deeper problems occur when there is a serious lack of alignment between cultural preferences and landscape resilience goals. What is the moral basis, for example, for biologists reintroducing wolves as a top predator in the landscape, and perhaps overriding the viewpoints of neighbouring landowners?

The key aesthetic problem concerning landscape connectivity is that it requires us to make value judgements about what we do in the wider countryside and urban green. We might admire the aesthetic qualities of a painting we own, hung on the wall of a house we own. However, if we admire a landscape, it generally belongs to other people, yet we want to influence what happens on their land. The aesthetics of landscape connectivity relate to complex and often non-visual processes above and below ground. They relate to manifold values and memories held by landscape 'insiders' and 'outsiders', based on the seen and unseen attributes of an area. The fundamental problem is, then, how can we legitimately intervene to achieve specific landscape-scale measures when the landscape is valued and owned by so many different interests?

One of the core concepts in helping us appreciate the nature of landscape-scale ethics is that of the 'ecological aesthetic'. An aspect of this is that we may aim to look beyond the prettiness of a particular landscape and, instead, see beauty in the way that it is functioning in a socially and ecologically resilient way (Carlson, 2007). Sometimes the two are entirely compatible. However, this is not always the case, not least because 'prettiness' is at least partly defined in terms of a shifting social consensus – for example, landscapes that have been sanitized by time may seem scenic and attractive now, but may have been viewed as poverty-stricken and violent places by a previous generation.

Gobster et al. (2007) have explored the links between aesthetics and landscape functionality. They note that landscape aesthetics provides a critical linkage between humans and ecological processes, because our sensory system is tied closely to our emotions and, of our emotions, pleasure has a fundamental influence on how we respond to the stimuli of our world. Further, aesthetic experience can drive landscape change, as we desire to see, live in and visit beautiful places and to avoid or want to improve places we perceive as ugly. This may, however, result in an excessively visual approach towards the landscape, referred to as the 'scenic aesthetic'. Even so, attention to ecological quality can be influenced by modifying our visual aesthetic value of landscapes. Understanding how people perceive and experience the beauty of all landscapes is central to achieving public support for, and compliance with, ecologically motivated landscape change. Gobster et al. appreciate that there will be tensions when human aesthetic preferences and ecological goals are not aligned – when what is seen as beautiful is deemed to be ecologically unhealthy or what is deemed to be ecologically healthy is seen as undistinguished or ugly. To address this dilemma, they invoke the concept of the ecological aesthetic for instances in which ecological processes may not conform to the visual qualities associated with a pleasurable landscape appearance. Without the acceptance of this broader aesthetic, there is a serious risk that the pursuit of tidiness and order – whether for amenity or economic production – might lead to ecologically damaging anthropogenic landscape change.

An important application of the ecological aesthetic is Nassauer's (1997) notion of 'intelligent care'. Fundamentally, there is no point in creating physical connections unless the landscape is then managed in a regenerative way. Much of our commercial management of landscapes is unsustainably exploitative; much of our management of leisure and amenity landscapes is unnecessarily fastidious and manicured. In advocating intelligent care, Nassauer was influenced by her perception of upper echelon residential environments in North America, where huge effort is often directed towards maintaining lawns and public open spaces in an excessively tidy, ornamental and artificial condition. Such a tradition has its place; however, in many instances there would be huge benefits for native biodiversity and other environmental attributes, as well as municipal budgets, in adopting less intrusive land-care approaches that were based on an intelligent and insightful appreciation of the landscape's natural dynamic. Hence, there is the possibility for society to cultivate the capacity to recognize landscapes that look ecologically resilient, and to appreciate their visual qualities. To our present eyes, such landscapes may sometimes look untidy or untended, yet if we apply a wisdom that perceives their inherent sustainability and resilience, we can both value them and learn to tend them appropriately – such an approach represents intelligent care. Nassauer draws upon Relph's (1981) concept of 'environmental humility' in this respect. She further advocates the concept of 'vivid care' where a benign human presence protects ecologically rich landscapes from less intelligent human control.

For some settings like publicly owned wildlands, aesthetic experiences and ecological goals are often in close alignment with each other – what looks good to people and provides valued aesthetic experiences also sustains ecological functions and processes. However, in other settings, aesthetic preferences may promote landscape change that undermines ecological goals. This may apply to urban landscaping, but it could equally well apply to excessive tidiness and control in farmed or forested landscapes, from which some people derive an aesthetic pleasure (Herrington, 2006). In these cases, landscape design, planning, policy and management activities may be used to bring aesthetic and ecological goals into closer alignment.

However, an ecological aesthetic is, by definition, 'normative' in that it asserts that it is desirable for humans to derive aesthetic pleasure from landscapes where nature is given a degree of free rein, rather than those where we appear to be in well ordered control. The underlying 'norm' is based on an assumption that aesthetic experiences can promote and sustain healthier ecosystems, and thus indirectly promote human health and welfare.

Yet when we make normative assumptions we cannot avoid implying that some people's views should prevail over others'. In the context of this book, the suggestion is that reconnection measures should be introduced by certain agents across landscapes that are valued and owned by many other people. For example, we might argue that a specialist ecological aesthetic should prevail over a popular scenic aesthetic, that local residents should be expected to accept increased flood risks in order to reinstate hydrological functionality, that restrictions should be placed on the economic activities of a landowner, or that tax revenues should be spent on subsidizing regional food products. This would not be a problem if planners and designers held a monopoly of wisdom, which clearly they do not. Nevertheless, as Gobster et al. (2007) note, policy, planning, design management and education are all inescapably normative activities – they are all ways in which a group of people seek to introduce changes that they judge to be improvements.

It is salutary to reflect further on the risks associated with normative assumptions. For example, one trap that we might fall into is to assume that local connections are good and global connections are bad. However, scenario development undertaken in the UK warns us against this type of essentialist thinking (Natural England, 2009d). Although the detail of these scenarios was not intended to be taken too literally, they present many ideas that challenge our image of the future. For example, a 'Connect for Life' scenario anticipated connection through vast global networks. Here, even though decisions and economies continued to be based locally, the emergence of billions of worldwide connections resulted in strong values and loyalties between dispersed communities of common purpose, whilst information and communication technologies contributed to productivity, social networking and Internet-enabled democratic decision making. Another scenario, 'Go for Growth', anticipated that making money would become a priority, with economic growth continuing to be driven by consumption and new technology, and society reacting to devastating events by spending money on food from abroad and accelerating technological innovation. A third scenario, 'Keep it Local' proposed that future society might revolve around nations feeding and providing for themselves, with land largely being used either for food production or for housing. Certain key decisions were made nationally, but most were made regionally and locally, and people became very protective of their local area and belongings. Resource use was tightly controlled but consumption remained high, environmental and resource limits started to be breached, and a series of social and environmental crises emerged, forcing nations to adopt more protectionist positions, slowing and unravelling globalization. Finally, a scenario of 'Succeed through Science' observed a booming global economy that relied on business-driven growth through scientific innovation, with a majority of stakeholders trusting that technology would enable growth within environmental and resource limits. Whilst the assumptions and outcomes of these scenarios can be contested,

Box 6.1 Key landscape-related themes emerging from scenarios about the future (based on Natural England, 2009d)

- Values take centre stage – there are debates about the ethic of care towards nature and the value attributable to nature for its own sake, despite all scenarios conceding in various degrees to a utilitarian view of nature, where the environment is seen as necessary to support lifestyles.
- Resources become constrained – both land and marine resources become more difficult to obtain (especially access to fresh water) so that all scenarios rely on new technologies to increase resource efficiency, though scenarios vary in their degree of self-sufficiency or reducing consumption.
- Identity and cohesion fragment – scenarios differ in the balance between global, national and local governance, and in the nature and role of cultural norms.
- Urban/rural distinctions blur – towns become greener and the countryside becomes more developed, with several scenarios producing policy-driven green infrastructure and the 'Keep it Local' scenario driving local food production.
- Economic growth and well-being diverge – wealth is variously seen as lying in land and natural resources, innovation and economic growth, and/or a healthier environment and social capital.
- Climate change stimulates varied responses – responses range from reactive adaptation to concerted international action, via defence of critical natural assets and acceptance of major lifestyle changes.
- Science and technology shape the future – the role of science and technology varies in terms of driving growth, using communication technologies to reduce travel, and ensuring national and resource security.
- Changes in food production alter land use – scenarios range from high-yield production and synthetic products focused on global food markets, to more traditional methods of producing food for immediate localities, with some high-technology solutions freeing up land for ecosystem services.

they are genuinely instructive about the risk of making normative and essentialist suppositions. Hyper-complex systems often behave counter-intuitively – unfavoured drivers can produce desired outcomes and vice versa. The study concluded that a number of themes would emerge during the future (Box 6.1): all of these appear to be contentious and there is not necessarily an obvious norm that should be adopted in each case, so great care must be taken when we seek to plan or design a particular outcome.

Broadly speaking, there is agreement that current practices and patterns of behaviour need to change if we are to meet the challenges of the future. However, choices about future landscapes are contentious – for example, whether wind turbines are welcome or unwelcome, whether sustainable drainage systems are sufficient to cope with future rainfall, whether forest cover should be greatly extended, or whether re-wilding is a desirable use of rural land. There is a risk of a 'nanny state' forcing trendy options on the public. Yet radical, evidence-based policies appear to be necessary, in which case a degree of normative thinking cannot be avoided. It is suggested here that norms can most safely be based on three principles. First, we can seek out underlying values and principles that have been widely debated, politically endorsed and appear to be part of a social consensus. This may not mean they are right, but it may at least give us a non-arbitrary basis on which to develop proposals. Second, we can improve the process of social and institutional learning, so that 'professional' and 'lay' interests are engaged in a shared discovery of the nature of key issues, and the ways in which they might successfully be addressed. Third, we can democratize the process as much as possible. When making decisions about landscape, we can develop deliberative processes for soliciting and incorporating the perspectives of multiple stakeholders and the wider public.

In seeking an underlying principle for landscape intervention, perhaps the most pertinent, widely endorsed meta-narrative of our age is that of 'sustainable development'. Although the concept of sustainability is itself contested, we have previously noted its principal dimensions in relation to landscape. A further check must be made in relation to social justice, because it would presently appear that the more disadvantaged sections of society are subject to greatest landscape hazard, for example in relation to paucity of green space (Pauleit et al., 2003), health (Mitchell and Popham, 2009) and flooding and pollution (Environment Agency, 2005). Broadly speaking, we could argue that landscape will best contribute to sustainable development when it becomes more adaptive and resilient in relation to future 'unknowns'. It is likely that this will entail reconnections that improve space for nature and place for people. Further, whilst planned and designed measures will be important, conditions can be created that permit landscapes the greatest opportunity for self-organization and emergence. This must, however, be set against the needs of a 'full-up' world to maintain decent standards of living without becoming excessively defensive and protectionist.

The role of shared learning, in which communities and institutions deliberate together to seek new options for sustainability, has also been discussed. The essence of this approach is to move away from the 'myth of the best argument' and to gain a better understanding of 'knowns and unknowns', so that more workable and widely accepted measures can be agreed. This also tends to produce communities that are more cognisant of the issues and more likely to revise their attitudes and behaviour. The role of expertise and the need for good science is still very central; however, experts need to move away from assuming a knowledge deficit amongst the public, towards one of co-discovery in complex and uncertain environmental conditions. This entails a broad commitment to social learning, which can often benefit from occurring in the situated, vivid setting of familiar landscapes. It also involves institutional learning amongst scientific and management agencies, not least in relation to the meanings and potentials of specific landscapes; and it requires a ripple effect of learning processes in communities of place, interest and practice. If it is conducted successfully, 'sustainability learning' is likely to generate outcomes that are more widely endorsed and therefore

Figure 6.1 Residents in the Dearne Valley, South Yorkshire, UK, create a frieze depicting past and future engagements with the river landscape (photo: Jill Selman)

more likely to achieve implementation and compliance, as well as be more scientifically grounded.

However, we have not yet given much attention to the third principle, namely, that of democratizing landscape options. Representative democracy clearly entails periodic elections as well as occasional referendums on issues of exceptional importance. However, it also depends on a range of continuous processes that solicit public opinions and incorporate these into policy and planning options in order to align them with social preferences (Figure 6.1). The participatory processes embedded in many spatial planning systems are an example of this.

Whilst all participatory processes raise significant practical and ethical issues, the incorporation of public preferences into landscape decisions faces a particular difficulty – namely, there is often no obviously preferable future direction for a given landscape. Although researchers have sought to gauge people's landscape preferences based on alternative future scenarios, these tend to be swayed by our predilection for the familiar, so that results tend to be quite predictable and conservative. They do not necessarily show how people might attach themselves to alternative landscapes or modify their view during a period of social learning. One expression of this dilemma has arisen during the various monitoring programmes of landscape change in England (Countryside Quality Counts, Character and Quality of England's Landscapes), which have sought to assess the nature of change relative to a baseline of current landscape character. Thus, it might be assumed that a

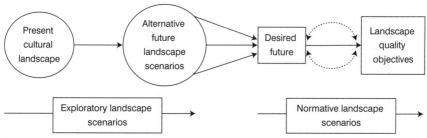

Figure 6.2 Building landscape quality objectives into future scenarios (adapted from Ramos, 2010)

suitable policy objective would be to maintain and enhance the distinctive qualities of an area. Monitoring, therefore, has concentrated on whether land use changes are neutral, reinforcing or conflictual in respect of existing character. However, whilst some changes may widely be agreed as undesirable, others might be entirely desirable and, indeed, the successful outcomes of deliberate policy – such as the transformation of the post-industrial character in England's National Forest. This is fundamentally different from, say, nature conservation objectives where there is a more obviously preferable direction, for example the increase in breeding success of a keystone species.

Thus, a central problem in democratizing landscape decisions lies in agreeing appropriate speeds and directions of change in individual landscapes. The main opportunity to achieve this is through what the European Landscape Convention (Council of Europe, 2000) has termed 'landscape quality objectives' (LQO), namely, 'the formulation by the competent public authorities of the aspirations of the public with regard to the landscape features of their surroundings'. This could clearly include urban landscapes and green infrastructure as well as countryside. The techniques for doing this remain under-developed, but a study by Ramos (2010) explored how the visions of the public should be conducted. Ramos looked in particular at rural landscapes where economic activities had been abandoned because they had become submarginal. In these rural landscapes the role of agriculture may have to assume different functions in the future. Thus the research conducted 'exploratory landscape scenarios' both to identify plausible futures, and to trigger discussions with the public regarding their aspirations for local landscapes. The methodological approach was illustrated through a case study of Mértola in south-east Portugal, where the researcher presented alternative scenarios to a range of experts, residents and other stakeholders. The exercise led to the development of futures that were perceived as plausible by local stakeholders and, thereby, able to expose their desires and concerns about the future of their landscape (Figure 6.2).

Jones (2007) has noted that such approaches towards integrating the public in the definition of LQOs should not be seen as a substitute for official

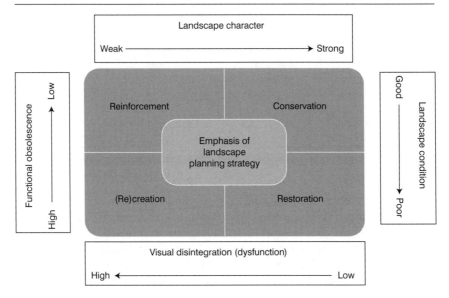

Figure 6.3 Alternative strategic emphases related to landscape character and condition (adapted from Warnock and Brown, 1998)

decision making, but as a complement to it. Thus, for example, 'integrated objectives' for landscape quality and ecosystem services have been identified for England's National Character Areas (Natural England, 2011), which will be used to guide planning processes and support for rural land managers. A popular approach in considering the desired future direction of a landscape is to appraise its existing condition and character and then decide whether the policy preference is for conservation of the present situation, reinforcement or adaptation of the most distinctive local qualities, restoration to a previous state, or creation of a new landscape (Warnock and Brown, 1998) (Figure 6.3).

The European Landscape Convention (ELC) implementation guidelines state that every planning action or project should comply with landscape quality objectives. In this way, developments should improve landscape quality, or at least not bring about a decline. One of the pioneering attempts to achieve this in an official governmental capacity as a response to the ELC requirement has been in Catalonia (Council of Europe, 2006). Here, the Act for the Protection, Planning and Management of the Landscape (2005) requires the setting of landscape quality objectives as a key point of reference for spatial and sectoral policies. Also, as well as influencing planning measures, LQOs have a function in increasing public awareness of the landscape and in the wider role of civil society. The principal instruments for defining LQOs have been a series of landscape catalogues prepared by the Catalan Landscape Observatory, and these set out the attributes, values and challenges identified in landscapes, based both on field evidence, and on

---

Box 6.2 Landscape quality objectives for Catalonia (adapted from Nogue, 2006)

1. Well preserved, planned and managed landscapes, of varied type (urban, suburban, rural or natural) and character.
2. Lively and dynamic landscapes – those existing and those newly created by intervention – capable of absorbing inevitable territorial transformations without losing their individuality.
3. Heterogeneous landscapes, reflecting the rich diversity of Catalan landscape and avoiding homogenization.
4. Orderly and harmonious landscapes, avoiding disruption and fragmentation.
5. Unique landscapes, anything but mundane.
6. Landscapes that retain and reinforce their references and values, both tangible and intangible (ecological, historical, aesthetic, social, productive, symbolic and identity-based).
7. Landscapes that are always respectful of the legacy of the past.
8. Landscapes that transmit tranquillity, free of dissonant elements, discordant sounds and light or odour pollution.
9. Landscapes that can be enjoyed without endangering their heritage and individuality.
10. Landscapes that take social diversity into account and contribute to the individual and social welfare of the population.

---

opinions gathered from the general public and the principal stakeholders. LQOs are defined for each distinct landscape character area.

The Catalan experience shows how LQOs represent the end result of a process comprising knowledge production, public consultation, policy formulation, and action and monitoring strategies. LQOs inform the preliminary guidelines for drawing up measures to protect and plan landscapes and manage them over time. They also link the social requirements and values attached to the landscape by the public to the choice of policy decisions made concerning the substance of the landscape components. Landscape quality objectives are defined in general landscape policy instruments for different scales (national, regional, local) and are formally implemented by spatial planning documents and sectoral instruments. From the long and varied list of landscape quality objectives that has emerged from this process, there are ten which consistently recur; we could suggest that these provide a normative basis for future landscape planning and management (Box 6.2).

Policy and practice for landscape connectivity

A key theme in this book has been the potential for future policy to promote a landscape that is joined-up, adaptive and resilient. Policies that aim to do this are more likely to be successfully implemented where their institutions 'learn' and acquire new capacity in order to respond to new situations in ways that are transparent and inclusive. Further, landscape policy is moving away from a sharp distinction between town and country, where rural protectionism or

Figure 6.4 Multiple ecosystem services in a connected urban landscape in Massachusetts, USA: the Back Bay Fens and Boston Common in Boston's 'Emerald Necklace'

urban 'landscaping' are the norm, to a more integrative focus on connective landscape systems (Selman, 2010b). Developmental processes are seen as possible drivers rather than just destroyers of emergent and multifunctional landscapes. The urban fringe, which has long been viewed as a problematic and undistinguished no-man's-land between real town and real countryside, is increasingly seen as the bridge to the countryside and the gateway to the town.

Policy for urban landscapes is starting to focus on the 'signatures' associated with the natural environment in towns and cities, as something integral to the planning and management of urban areas. It has been suggested that the distinctive fabric of the natural environment in towns and cities makes a major contribution to urban landscape and sense of place, underpins the adaptation of urban areas to a rapidly changing climate, and provides environmental security for communities. It creates opportunities to access high quality natural environment in urban areas in order to enjoy a wide range of environmental and social benefits. Implementation clearly needs to address the complex institutional and landownership structure of cities, and the challenges posed by loss of community and casual attitudes towards the environment. However, there is also great potential as large portions of cities are not built on, and include parks and gardens, amenity green spaces, allotments, areas of 'encapsulated' countryside, streams and road verges. These natural areas are already delivering multiple ecosystem services such as rainwater drainage and harvesting, temperature regulation, air filtration, food products and noise reduction (Figure 6.4).

As an example, the London Regional Landscape Framework (Baxter, 2011) aims to reconnect Londoners with the underlying nature of the city, and to see landscapes as being integral to the capital's character. The results have shown how landscape character types cut across Borough boundaries, revealing the artificiality of administrative units, and the more fundamental reality that underlies systemic ecosystem services. Thus, despite centuries of urbanization, areas still betray a distinctive 'natural signature', revealed through a range of landscape qualities and functions (Gill et al., 2009). However, there is currently little awareness of the city's underlying nature, and this has been a major cause of the erosion of its natural character. The natural signature approach is being used as a planning and policy basis to achieve greater resilience and reconnection in the capital. This approach also bears similarities to the emerging field of landscape urbanism, which suggests that it is the intrinsic potential within cities' underlying landscape systems that fundamentally imparts 'place-ness' to the urban realm (Waldheim, 2006).

In more rural contexts, landscape policy is moving away from a predominantly protectionist approach aimed at the finest landscapes, important though these may be as cultural treasures and exemplars of sustainable development. Instead, policy is increasingly concerned to rebalance efforts between 'fine' and 'everyday' landscapes. This is combined with an acceptance not only of the inevitability of rural landscape change, but also of the need for an improved understanding of the nature of change in order to realize positive opportunities for the proactive planning and management of landscape evolution (Natural England, 2010). Thus, rural landscapes are not considered to be frozen at a point in time, but rather that policies can help to steer their evolution in ways that support a continuing distinctiveness and functionality. In turn, this requires policy makers to develop an understanding of what society will want from future landscapes, to find effective ways of guiding and influencing change, and to reflect these in forward-looking landscape quality objectives. Indeed, this policy perspective sees landscapes as providing the basic spatial and temporal framework through which changes are organized, planned and managed. As with urban areas, there is a core challenge in achieving the effective and positive engagement of landowners and land managers, and collaboration between local authorities, local communities, statutory agencies, the voluntary and private sectors, farmers, other land managers and individual citizens (Lawton et al., 2010).

Trends in rural policy (HM Government, 2011) currently suggest mainstreaming the value of nature to society, particularly through the promotion of a green economy in which markets better reflect the value of nature. There is also a recognition that past policy action has often taken place on too small a scale, and that it is now important to promote an integrated approach, based on resilient natural networks, in order to move from a situation of net loss to net gain in ecosystem services (Box 6.3).

Moving from policy to practice, the current term of preference for space- and place-making in the wider landscape is that of 'green infrastructure' (GI), with the implication that this also includes the 'blue infrastructure' of streams, wetlands and sustainable drainage systems. Tzoulas et al. (2007) argue that the concept of GI is a basis for upgrading the urban green to be a single, coherent planning entity. They argue that GI can be considered to comprise all natural, semi-natural and artificial networks of multifunctional ecological

Box 6.3 Selected proposals for landscape connection in government policy (summarized from HM Government, 2011)

In relation to joined-up networks and resilient spaces:

- Establishing Local Nature Partnerships, which would enable local leadership and could operate across administrative boundaries, be integrated with economic development mechanisms, and would raise awareness about the services and benefits of a healthy natural environment.
- Creating Nature Improvement Areas (NIAs) to enhance and reconnect nature on a significant scale, again supported by local partnerships.
- Reforming the planning system to take a strategic approach to planning for nature within and across local areas, guiding development to preferred locations, encouraging greener design and enabling development to enhance natural networks (e.g. through 'biodiversity offsets').
- Promoting concerted action across farmed land, woodlands and forests, towns and cities, and rivers and water bodies.

In relation to reconnecting people and nature:

- Capitalizing on the positive impact that nature has on mental and physical health, the effect that high quality natural environments have on healthy neighbourhoods, the effect of green spaces in encouraging social activity and reducing crime, and the role of the natural environment in helping children's learning.
- Promoting voluntary activity to improve wildlife habitats or remove litter, and enabling people to make well-informed choices in their everyday lives (e.g. as shoppers, householders and gardeners), which are felt to encourage the emergence of connections that are good for people and nature.
- Making nature enhancement a central goal of social action across the country through a variety of measures in local government, health authorities, schools and community action.

systems within urban and peri-urban areas, at all spatial scales, characterized by their quality, quantity, multifunctionality and interconnectedness. Thus, GI delivery in urban and rural environments is seen as a way of delivering a range of ecosystem services through a strategic and local network that has quality and integrity. These services include: climate change mitigation and adaptation; safeguarding and encouraging biodiversity; economic productivity; food and energy security; public health and well-being; social cohesion; reconnecting people with the natural environment; sustainable use of a finite land resource; and the importance of place-making in sustainable communities (Landscape Institute, 2009). Further, the functions are seen to be interactive and synergistic in terms of catalyzing a range of other socially desirable goals (Table 6.1).

Various organizations have now responded by producing GI guides for developers. For example, one subregional agency in south-eastern England has affirmed GI as critical infrastructure that needs to be embedded at the start of projects. Their planning guidance identifies a range of different

Table 6.1 Relating GI 'services' to social policy priorities (adapted from Landscape Institute, 2009)

	Policy priorities					
	Economic – sustainable growth and employment	Environmental – protection of heritage, biodiversity and geodiversity	Environmental – landscape modification and creation	Environmental – climate change mitigation and adaptation	Social – active transport	Social – health, well-being, social capital
Access, recreation, engagement	✓	✓			✓	✓
Habitat provision, accessible in nature		✓	✓	✓		✓
Landscape setting and context for development	✓	✓	✓			
Energy production and conservation	✓			✓		
Productive landscapes	✓	✓		✓	✓	✓
Flood and water resource management	✓		✓	✓		✓
Equable microclimates	✓			✓		✓

Box 6.4 Different types of green space that can be integrated into green infra-structure (Sources: based on information in Landscape Institute, 2009; and Chris Blandford Associates, 2010)

Types of green space asset:

- Parks and gardens – urban parks, pocket parks, country and regional parks, formal gardens and country estates.
- Amenity green space – informal recreation spaces, children's play areas, playing fields, communal green spaces within housing areas, domestic gardens, village greens, urban commons, other incidental space and green roofs.
- Natural and semi-natural green spaces – woodland and scrub, nature reserves, grassland, heath and moor, wetlands, open water bodies and running water, wastelands and disturbed ground, and bare rock habitats.
- Green corridors – rivers/canals including their banks, road and rail corridors/verges, hedgerows, ditches, cycling routes, pedestrian paths and rights of way.
- Other green space – allotments, community gardens, city farms, cemeteries and churchyards, registered commons, village and town greens, heritage sites, development sites with potential for open space and links, land in agri-environmental management.

Types of green space asset characterized by landscape scale:

Regional and national scale	City and district scale	Local and neighbourhood scale
national and regional parks	business settings	street trees, verges, hedges
national landscape designations	city/ district/ country parks	green roofs and walls
rivers, floodplains, shorelines	urban canals and rivers	pocket parks, village greens, commons
long-distance trails and greenways	urban commons/ forests	churchyards, cemeteries
forests and woodlands	lakes/ waterfronts/ floodplains	rights of way, cycle routes
reservoirs	agricultural land/ allotments/ city farms	ponds, streams, swales, ditches
road, railway and canal networks	recycled brownfield land and landfill sites	sports pitches, play areas, school grounds
agricultural land	regional landscape and wildlife designations	local nature reserves
green belts		private gardens, community gardens, allotments
		vacant and derelict land

types of green space that can be strategically combined into a coherent infrastructure. These comprise areas in public and private ownership, with and without public access, and in both urban and rural locations (Chris Blandford Associates, 2010) (Box 6.4).

Achieving an effective and integrated GI that is more than the sum of its parts will require the pursuit of 'regenerative design' within both existing and *de novo* situations. In other words, there are some occasions where a completely new land use is proposed – such as creation of an ecotown, plantation of a forest or the large-scale reclamation of a former industrial area – and other situations where GI must be retrofitted into an existing urban area or farming system. An approach to how this might be achieved in the context of urban design has been proposed by Lovell and Johnston (2009), who suggest that urban performance can be transformed by integrating ecological principles into landscape design. They challenge the conventional assumption of landscape ecology that presumes that ecological quality in the human-dominated matrix is poor. By focusing on the development of multifunctional landscapes, guided by the rapidly growing knowledge base of ecosystem services provided by landscape features, they demonstrate how the spatial heterogeneity of the urban landscape can be improved through the addition of semi-natural landscape elements. Whilst these elements may, individually, be small they may be collectively important, especially where intentionally designed and connected. The authors show how specific provisioning, regulation and cultural ecosystem services can be promoted through the establishment of an integrated system of elements such as: patches of native vegetation; vegetative buffers; natural or constructed wetlands; edible gardens; storm water infiltration systems; and waste treatment systems. At the wider urban scale, the Town and Country Planning Association (2004) proposed the promotion of a strategic green infrastructure of regional parks, green grids, community forests, natural green spaces and greenway linkages.

An example of the strategic pursuit of GI is provided by the East London Green Grid (Natural England, 2009b). Whilst London is one of the greenest capitals in the world with a large number of parks and leafy suburbs, some areas of east London are severely deficient in green spaces – 22 per cent of east Londoners do not have access to a regional park, a third of the area does not have a local park within 400 metres (m) of people's homes, and extensive areas lack a dedicated wildlife site. The East London Green Grid therefore aims to create a network of interlinked, multipurpose open spaces with good connections to the areas where people live and work, as well as to the green belt and the River Thames. The Grid includes rural areas where ecosystem services can be promoted through agri-environment schemes, as well as more obviously urban areas where master planning and regeneration schemes become important. It also links to wider policy initiatives such as a 'Walking the Way to Health' scheme targeted at areas of social deprivation and Climate Change Adaptation Plans. Overall, the Green Grid aims to:

- provide new and enhance existing public open spaces, whilst reducing areas of deficiency;
- provide public access along the Thames tributaries and green networks;
- provide a range of formal and informal recreational uses and landscapes, thereby promoting healthy living;
- provide new and enhance existing wildlife sites;
- manage water collection and flood risk via multifunctional spaces;
- combat the effects of the urban heat island;

- provide beautiful, diverse and managed green infrastructure to the highest standards for people and wildlife.

An approach commonly taken in the USA is to allow developers latitude in designing an imaginative green infrastructure for their master plans. Rather than precisely specifying a rigid layout, overall proportions of developed and undeveloped land are set, and then scope is given to alter housing densities in order to consolidate green areas into meaningful clusters. Latimer and Hill (2008) note the advantages of this process of 'mitigation banking' (also known as 'biodiversity offset'), which involves acquiring and retaining land in advance for ecological mitigation required by subsequent development, especially where it is established in the regulatory framework. Typically, the mitigation bank is established by acquiring land for the creation, or enhancement and management, of habitats or ecosystems for a particular wildlife or environmental resource. The asset can be valued in terms of credits (similar to carbon trading) and the better the condition of the land in terms of its environmental objectives, the greater its value. Land may be acquired by financial institutions, businesses, landowners or investors and managed to maximize its biodiversity/environmental capital. Credits may then be sold as the land develops into the appropriate and stable condition for which the asset was purchased. The results of mitigation banking are broadly positive, and its main weaknesses in practice tend to relate to poor regulatory supervision rather than to the approach itself. However, some people are concerned that biodiversity offsets might be used as an excuse by developers to enable them to destroy good quality habitat in return for vague promises of creating variable quality habitat elsewhere. Thus, it will only tend to work positively where developers accord with specific principles, namely:

- Like-for-like mitigation – the principle of no-net-loss requires credits that are in keeping with the scale of loss and the nature of the loss.
- Critical natural capital or non-replaceable habitats – mitigation banks are limited to those habitats that can be created or manipulated to increase their conservation value, and exclude existing key sites.
- Spatial relationships between development areas and mitigation sites – new sites must reflect criteria of size (e.g. create large areas at a landscape scale rather than small isolated sites), location (favourably located and possibly within the same character area) and timescales (if planning rules permit, create new areas well in advance of loss) (Latimer and Hill, 2008).

For example, Taylor et al. (2007) referred to a zoning ordinance in Fenton Township, Michigan, that encouraged the preservation of open space within the developable portion of a site in exchange for increased residential densities elsewhere on the site. Although the approach had merit, they found that current practice paid too little attention to the effective definition of natural features, gave too little legal safeguard for their protection, and lacked a clear spatial context for design decisions. The authors presented ideas to the planning authority as to how the situation could be improved so that the adopted policies could be achieved more effectively. In a UK context, it has officially been recognized that biodiversity offsets should not be seen as an alternative to the strong protection of important habitat, but as a complementary way of helping to expand and restore the wider ecological network. Used in a strategic way they might help to deliver more, better, bigger and joined-up networks of habitat. In addition to the principles noted above, UK policy also proposes a further one – 'additionality' – so that offsets are required to deliver conservation outcomes that are additional to those that would have occurred anyway (HM Government, 2011).

One of the key concerns in designing and managing GI is the lack of skills in delivering such a complex and highly interactive system. Most of our experience has been with grey infrastructure, which, despite its high degree of sophistication, is still generally mono-functional (e.g. a supersized storm water pipe) and within the competence of a clearly defined profession (e.g. civil engineering). By contrast, GI is multifunctional and requires an understanding of an entire working landscape. However, in a survey of fifty-four UK local authorities, 68 per cent said a lack of specific landscape skills was affecting overall service delivery (Commission for Architecture and the Built Environment, 2010). Beyond a particular expertise in landscape, there is a more general need for GI managers with expertise in partnership working and leadership who can break down the silos between traditional 'sectors' such as green space and water management, transport planning, children's play, nature conservation and local food production. In contrast to most current situations, leaders would need to be in a sufficiently senior position to provide the comprehensive management needed to deliver an integrated network of GI across an area. Not surprisingly, a number of significant barriers have been identified to effective GI implementation (Box 6.5).

As noted, delivering GI is not just a question of designing a network, but also of developing partnerships that possess sufficient institutional thickness to ensure effective implementation and care. One organization has advocated a four-stage process (North West Green Infrastructure Think Tank, 2009; North West Green Infrastructure Unit, 2009; North West Climate Change Partnership, 2011) to achieve this. First, the stage of 'data audit and resource mapping' builds up a data resource of available information including maps, regional and national guidance, data sets, relevant policy frameworks, regional and national strategies and stakeholders. This information is synthesized into a Geographic Information System (GIS) map of the area showing GI types and locations. Second, partners undertake a 'functional assessment' of the existing GI in terms of the ecosystem services that it is

---

Box 6.5 Potential barriers to the implementation of GI (adapted from Landscape Institute, 2009)

- lack of the right kinds of expertise, compounded by local government outsourcing of contracts that has led to a de-skilling of green space workforces;
- an increasingly urbanized society that has become detached from the natural environment, and sees it basically as a place to be visited rather than an integral part of daily life;
- inadequate investment in the long-term management of GI assets, resulting from a culture of short-term thinking;
- lack of investment in GI before growth occurs, as planning gain following development is often insufficient;
- administrative boundaries artificially constraining the area that needs to be considered for effective GI implementation;
- a standards-based approach to open space that has, in the past, tended to place undue emphasis on quantity rather than quality and on single use land allocations rather than rich, multifunctional green space;
- inadequate quantification of the full economic benefits to be gained from investment in GI, compounded by a lack of commitment and understanding from private sector bodies.

---

currently delivering, where it is functioning well and needs to be maintained, and where it needs to be improved. The future situation is assessed in terms of threats to the GI, location of opportunities for improvement and ways of securing future change. Third, a 'needs assessment' is required, cross-referencing the GI plan with other strategic programmes, and identifying its impact in relation to wider social and economic data such as deprivation indices. Finally, the partners need to agree an 'intervention plan', seeking positive environmental changes while taking into account a range of related issues such as local character and resources, and determining the types of regulatory, incentive-based and direct physical interventions required.

The successful use of a partnership approach to joined-up action is also evidenced in projects funded through the UK Heritage Lottery Fund's Landscape Partnerships programme (Cumulus, 2009). This programme grant-aided landscape-scale projects within areas of distinctive character. Working at this scale led to more holistic and better integrated heritage management, enabled habitats to be dealt with as a whole, and catalyzed wider sustainable development benefits. It also led partners to take a wider view of landscape that contributed to the sustainability of projects and activities, and had spill-over effects into adjoining areas. Delivering the programme on a partnership basis also created numerous practical advantages as well as engaging whole communities and sectors rather than just individuals.

One of the key purposes of GI is to reconnect people and their local landscape. In this regard, one study (Ray and Moseley, 2007) used the previously discussed 'forest habitat network' approach to assess whether it may be possible to integrate the needs of people and wildlife in green networks within urban environments. The approach used a landscape ecological algorithm known as the least cost focal species approach – in other words, a model that assumes that selected representative species will use the landscape in ways that minimize their energy 'cost' of spatial behaviour – as a way of mapping and analysing urban networks. The approach is usually only applied to wild species, but a particularly novel aspect of this study involved the treatment of humans as a focal species by creating three profiles to represent (1) low range users who are currently less likely to engage with green space; (2) medium range 'average' users; and (3) high range, active and confident people who readily use a variety of green space types. It also defined biodiversity (wild species) groups on the basis of local assessments reflecting sites that were excellent, above average and average. Thus the approach expressed the current and potential networks for both people and biodiversity. The networks indicate that, whilst the green space areas are accessible to high range users, other user types, particularly low range users, are limited in range or may lack access as they do not have (or are unwilling to get to) nearby green space. The model outputs could be used to target green space improvements so as to meet a range of policy objectives including health, social inclusion, biodiversity improvement, SuDS and sustainable transport. Implementation, though, is likely to entail compromises between social needs, which are often the major driver for green space development in urban areas, and biodiversity improvement. However, the study was able to propose a number of practical ways forward, not least in the light of regulatory provisions such as the Habitats and Species Regulations 2010 that encourage land development policies to support landscape features that perform an ecological 'stepping stone' role (Box 6.6).

In a more rural context, the Living Landscapes initiative of the UK's non-governmental conservation sector (The Wildlife Trusts, 2009) sets out principles for restoring a green network for the benefit of wildlife and people. The proposals are pitched at a 'landscape scale' and take a forward-looking approach to biodiversity. Thus, in addition to conventional backward-looking protectionist measures, the programme seeks to: understand nature, appreciate it and work with it; understand the processes that give rise to habitats, and provide conditions suitable for key species; understand how these processes can be influenced or copied; see wildlife and nature as synonymous with natural processes, and ecological functioning; and understand the interaction between cultural and natural landscape. The strategy proposes that if a habitat unit is to be self-sufficient in all its typical species, then all structural types and stages, and hence the niches they provide, must be present all the time. In order to achieve this, the proposals are based on the concept of minimum dynamic area (MDA), which is the smallest area that can possess a natural disturbance regime that maintains internal recolonization sources and thereby minimizes extinction. In other

---

Box 6.6 Potential ways of securing forest habitat networks (based on Ray and Moseley, 2007)

- Encouraging planners and developers to seize opportunities to add new woodland and protect existing woodland, safeguard biodiversity, mitigate the impact of climate change and improve community landscapes.
- Requiring woodland planting on development sites to be substantial, noting that 150 m width will eventually provide 50 m of core woodland conditions, which is the minimum recommended size for new woodland.
- Endeavouring to achieve accessible natural green space targets in new developments – for example accessibility to woodlands of 2 ha or more within 500 m of where people live.
- Expanding high quality woodland by planting contiguous patches, and protecting it from development by an ecologically appropriate buffer zone at least 250 m wide, in order to provide a more natural environment for communities, help reduce disturbance to biodiversity and minimize the woodland edge effect on core woodland species.
- Targeting woodlands containing high quality compartments for consolidation and expansion, with the surrounding low quality woodland being improved to provide a range of woodland conditions for species dispersing from the high quality compartments.
- Actively managing ancient woodland sites where they are in poor condition, and targeting the restoration of areas of former ancient woodland on cleared or replanted sites where four or more ancient woodland indicator species are still present.
- Expanding woodland by selecting tree species suited to local habitat type based on ecological site classifications.
- Targeting woodlands of currently low biodiversity quality for structural management, to improve their condition and encourage a greater number and diversity of woodland species.

---

words, it is the smallest area required for a species or habitat to sustain itself independently without intervention. Methods to establish MDA include assuring a core area in order to prevent habitat fragmentation, and promoting resilience by ensuring that a given unit of a habitat is considerably larger than the size of the largest predictable disturbance event. For example, a small patch of heathland would be subject to enormous fluctuations in structure and composition over time if all stages of heathland growth were to be wiped out in a single fire event. The strategy thus incorporates the assumption that the size of a functional unit of a habitat is determined by the area needed to support a stable breeding population of its most area-demanding species.

Central to the success of the Living Landscapes initiative is its intention to fit landscape-scale conservation areas into existing features. Thus, in densely populated areas it is generally not possible to establish giant nature reserves, and so habitat patches will need to exist alongside, around and in between villages, agricultural land and other land uses. The most realistic aim is to seek a minimum degree of interconnectedness between patches by building around existing high quality clusters, from which habitat can expand. It is argued that this should progressively build a resilient landscape by reversing the trend towards small, isolated habitat fragments that effectively act as sinks, and by reconnecting fragments that act as source areas with self-sustaining populations of species from which recolonization of the surrounding landscape can occur. Overall, therefore, the Living Landscapes strategy is based on 'restore, recreate, reconnect' in order to rebuild biodiversity on a landscape scale, based upon the best potential areas.

Embedding a joined-up landscape approach at the national scale is well evidenced by the Estonian 'network of ecologically compensating areas' (Külvik, and Sepp, 2007). This programme has developed from the east European 'ecostabilizing' concept that was initially developed during the era of state socialism (Hawkins and Selman, 2002). In this, a multifunctional approach to ecological networks is based on a strong land use planning tradition, with wilderness and areas of conservation value as core areas, interlinked by natural and semi-natural landscapes. Latterly, in Estonia, the spatial planning system has progressed the ecostabilization concept as a green network. This simplifies the complex theoretical problems of ecological networks and concentrates, instead, on demarcating a network with characteristics that are mappable and deliverable in terms of planning practice, and which also have socio-economic relevance. Thus, the network is attractive to landscape architects and land use planners for channelling recreation and identifying ecological corridors, especially in areas close to settlements. According to the Estonian Spatial Plan the green network is a coherent system of extensively used areas in a comparatively good natural state that helps to maintain the biodiversity and stability of the environment. The country's Environmental Action Plans have been used to promote the methodology of green network planning, and the development of complementary economic data sets and specialist education. The national planning 'vision' contains a chapter and schematic map on green networks, which determines the total network coverage at around 55 per cent of the national territory, in twelve comparatively compact core areas. This area is large enough not only to fulfil the compensatory function at a national level, but also on a European scale. The planning system is then able to seek solutions to the key problems of anthropogenic load on the green network – notably, maintaining the ecological network in regions of high human activity in the vicinity of settlements and highways, and maintaining the continuity of networks in places where highways penetrate the large compensatory areas (Külvik and Sepp, 2007).

The green network is addressed at all levels in the spatial planning hierarchy, namely, country (national plan), counties (county plans) and municipalities (comprehensive plans). Thus, the national long-term spatial plan – 'Estonia 2010' – delineates the basic principles of the network by establishing corridors and twelve core areas of national and international importance. At a county level, the green network is a sub-theme of spatial planning that aims to define environmental conditions for the development of land use and settlement, and to identify their valuable cultural/historic landscapes. In this regard, each of the country's fifteen counties has been required to prepare a map of ecological networks on a scale of 1:50,000, as one of the layers of thematic spatial planning. At the municipality level, legislation requires the delineation of the boundaries of the green network, and requirements for land use within it, to be included as a topic in the comprehensive plan. This general approach is now spreading amongst other countries and regions.

Until now, landscape planning has been a generally spatial affair, framed in two dimensions across the surface area of land. Especially as the world becomes predominantly urbanized, we are having to give more attention to three dimensions, and to the 'stacked' landscape. Key examples are the vertical farm (Despommier, 2010), and the creation of multifunctional green spaces on roofs (Dunnett and Kingsbury, 2008) and walls (Blanc, 2008). Although the notion of the vertical farm remains contentious, it is almost certain that the three-dimensional potential of the city to contribute to feeding the growing urban population will be realized in the future – by 2050, it is expected that 80 per cent of the world's population will live in cities. Variants range from quite long-established techniques with hydroponics and glasshouses, to hermetic artificial environments stacked as skyscrapers. Proponents argue that vertical farming can reduce food miles and meet the urgent human needs of megacities, as well as reducing the demand on rural agriculture, allowing it to become less intensive. Because it is based on self-contained systems, it can efficiently recycle wastes. Opponents have questioned the economics of the vertical farms, in terms of massive start-up and substantial operating costs, as well as their potential exacerbation of light and air pollution. There are also unresolved questions about whether they can operate on renewable energy sources alone, or require subsidies from conventional sources. The arguments in favour of vertical green space are, in contrast, well established and widely practised. A key argument in their favour is their potential for mitigating urban discomfort from climate change. We earlier considered the role of surface green space in moderating future temperatures and flood hazard, but models point to the substantial additional contribution of green roofs and walls (Foster et al., 2011). Bruse and Skinner (2000), for example, undertook a study of Melbourne in which they modelled the effects of greening on urban microclimate, by comparing the effects of adding either surface vegetation or rooftop vegetation, and of adding both of them together ('all greened' scenario). The 'all-greened' case produced significant additional benefits because it appeared that the green spaces effectively combined in ways that produced more uniform, rather than just local, effects on pedestrian comfort, especially in relation to cooling, shading and shelter from wind.

Relatively little information is available on connective strategies below ground but research into the hyporheic zone – the saturated zone beneath a stream that contains water derived from the stream – demonstrates the importance of understanding its links with surface waters. Valett et al. (1994) showed how downwelling stream water supplies dissolved oxygen, nutrients and organic matter to the ecological communities in the hyporheos, whereas upwelling water can influence river ecology by supplying surface waters that have a distinctive water chemistry. This, in consequence, influences in-stream biota by enhancing the diversity of surface water habitat. More recently, Kondolf et al., 2006) have demonstrated that, despite these interactions, strategies for river rehabilitation rarely explicitly consider the hyporheic zone or seek to restore lost vertical linkages with groundwater.

Although three-dimensional strategies for landscape-scale reconnection are still only at the embryonic stage it seems likely that they will grow in importance. Now that the majority of the world's population lives in towns and cities, and will become rapidly more urbanized during the twenty-first century, it is probable that the emphasis of landscape planning will tip from rural to urban. This is likely to lead us to pursuing vertical, as well as horizontal, options for sustainability and resilience.

Conclusion

This book has suggested that, not only is systematic landscape reconnection desirable, but also that there are numerous examples of how this can be achieved in the future. It has proposed an approach that links policy and practice to the emergence of more sustainable and resilient landscapes (Figure 6.5). However, there are two major problems. One is conceptual, and concerns the ways that we think about the landscape, as well as the likelihood that social preferences for the use of landscapes might conflict with those of private landowners. The other is practical – how to agree policies and devise effective implementation mechanisms that succeed in joining up physical systems across wide areas that are in multiple landownership.

There is no easy solution to the ethical problems of large-scale landscape intervention. Not least, is the difficulty of finding agreement about collective courses of action, especially where aesthetic preferences conflict with developers' or scientists' recommendations. One possibility is to base our options on political principles that have been subjected to widespread and transparent debate, and which command extensive support. Pre-eminently, in contemporary society, the axiom of sustainability seems to fulfil this need. Hence, the pursuit of landscape options that demonstrably contribute to sustainable development is one way of justifying intervention. Alongside this, it is important to debate landscape quality objectives, underpinned by opportunities for social and institutional learning. These provide a clearly articulated basis for pursuing specific landscape options in particular localities.

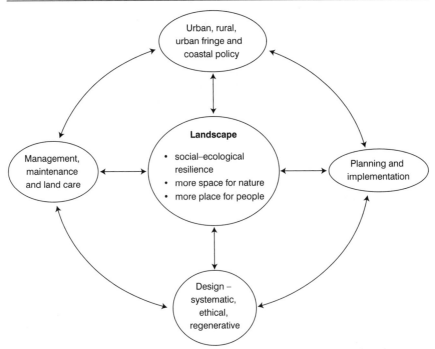

Figure 6.5 Arenas for pursuing landscape connectedness through improved policy, planning, design and management

Although the pursuit of landscape reconnection over whole cities and tracts of countryside might seem administratively daunting, numerous successes have already been achieved. There are clear principles and mechanisms, as well as documented case studies, which indicate the scope for physical reconnection. Opportunities exist both in relation to the two-dimensional space of the landscape surface, and to the three-dimensional space of physical layers above and below ground. The landscape commands an important place in the psyche of most nations. However, there is a risk that nostalgia for traditional and imagined landscapes can pose a barrier to the emergence of new landscapes that are resilient and adaptive. This book suggests that social reconnection with landscape, and the creation of social capacity to drive sustainable landscape change, can promote the emergence of future landscapes that are reconnected, resilient and cherished.

References

Adams, W. M. (2003) *Future Nature: A Vision for Nature Conservation*. London: Earthscan.

Ahern, J. (1995) 'Greenways as a planning strategy', *Landscape and Urban Planning*, 33: 131–155.

Bartens, J. and The Mersey Forest Team (2009) *Green Infrastructure and Hydrology*. Warrington: The Mersey Forest.

Bauer, N., Wallner, A. and Hunziker, M. (2009) 'The change of European landscapes: human-nature relationships, public attitudes towards rewilding, and the implications for landscape management in Switzerland', *Journal of Environmental Management*, 90: 2910–2920.

Baxter (Alan Baxter Associates) (2011) *London's Natural Signatures: The London Landscape Framework*. London: Alan Baxter Associates.

Beckwith, M.E. and Gilster, S.D. (1997) 'The paradise garden: a model garden design for those with Alzheimer's disease', *Activities, Adaptation and Aging*, 22: 3–16.

Bennett, G. and Mulongoy, K. J. (2006) *Review of Experience with Ecological Networks, Corridors and Buffer Zones*. Montreal: Secretariat of the Convention on Biological Diversity, Technical Series No. 23.

Berkes, F. and Folke, C. (eds) (1998) *Linking Social and Ecological Systems: Management Practices and Social Mechanisms for Building Resilience*. New York: Cambridge University Press.

Bird, W. (2007) *Natural Thinking*. Report to the Royal Society for the Protection of Birds. Sandy, Bedfordshire: RSPB.

Blanc, P. (2008) *Le Mur Végétal, de la nature à la ville* ('The green wall in town and country'). Neuilly-sur-Seine: éditions Michel Lafon.

Bolliger, J., Sprott, J. C. and Mladenoff, D. J. (2003) 'Self-organization and complexity in historical landscape patterns', *Oikos*, 100: 541–553.

Bourdieu, P. (1997) 'The forms of capital', in A. H. Halsey, H. Lauder, P. Brown and A. Stuart Wells (eds) *Education: Culture, Economy, Society*, Oxford: Oxford University Press.

Bradley, D., Bradley, J., Coombes, M. and Tranos, E. (2009) *Sense of Place and Social Capital and the Historic Built Environment*. Newcastle: University of Newcastle, International Centre for Cultural and Heritage Studies.

Broadmeadow, M. S. J., Webber, J. F., Ray, D. and Berry, P. M. (2009) 'An assessment of likely future impacts of climate change on UK forests', in D. J. Read, P. H. Freer-

Smith, J. I. L. Morison, N. Hanley, C. C. West, and P. Snowdon (eds) *Combating Climate Change – A Role for UK Forests. An assessment of the potential of the UK's trees and woodlands to mitigate and adapt to climate change.* Edinburgh: The Stationery Office.

Brummel, R. F., Nelson, K. C., Grayzeck Souter, S., Jakes, P. J. and Williams D. R. (2010) 'Social learning in a policy-mandated collaboration: community wildfire protection planning in the eastern United States', *Journal of Environmental Planning and Management*, 53: 681–699.

Bruse, M. and Skinner, C. J. (2000) *Rooftop Greening and Local Climate: A Case Study in Melbourne.* Biometeorology and Urban Climatology at the Turn of the Millennium, WMO/TD No. 1026, Geneva: World Meteorological Organization.

BTCV (2002) *Well-being Comes Naturally: Evaluation of the Portslade Green Gym. Research Summary.* Doncaster: British Trust for Conservation Volunteers.

Burt, T. P. and Pinay, G. (2005) 'Linking hydrology and biogeochemistry in complex landscapes', *Progress in Physical Geography*, 29: 297–316.

Cantrill, J. G. and Senecah, S. L. (2001) 'Using the "sense of self-in-place" construct in the context of environmental policy-making and landscape planning', *Environmental Science and Policy*, 4: 185–203.

Carlson, A. (2007) 'On aesthetically appreciating human environments', in A. Berleant and A. Carlson (eds) *The Aesthetics of Human Environments.* Buffalo, NY: Broadview Press.

Castells, M. (1983) *The City and the Grassroots: A Cross-cultural Theory of Urban Social Movements.* Berkeley, CA: University of California Press.

Chartered Institution of Water and Environmental Management (CIWEM) (2010) *Multi-functional Urban Green Infrastructure.* London: CIWEM.

Chris Blandford Associates (2010) *A guide for sustainable communities in Milton Keynes South Midlands: Adding Value to Development.* London: Chris Blandford Associates.

Christopherson, R. W. (1997) *Geosystems: An Introduction to Physical Geography.* Upper Saddle River, NJ: Prentice-Hall.

Clarke, L. (2010) *Delivering green infrastructure in the existing urban environment.* Briefing note. London: Construction Industry Research and Information Association.

Commission for Architecture and the Built Environment (CABE) (2010) *Grey to Green: How we Shift Funding and Skills to Green Our Cities.* London: CABE.

Commission for Architecture and the Built Environment (CABE) (n.d.) http:// webarchive.nationalarchives.gov.uk/20110118095356/http:/www.cabe.org.uk/ sustainable-places/advice/urban-food-production (accessed 6 February 2012).

Conservation Fund (2004) *Green Infrastructure — Linking Lands for Nature and People.* Case Study 2: Florida's Ecological Network, Arlington, VA: The Conservation Fund.

Cooper-Marcus, C. and Barnes, M. (eds) (1999) *Healing Gardens: Therapeutic Benefits and Design Recommendations.* New York: John Wiley.

Council of Europe (2000) *The European Landscape Convention.* Strasbourg: Council of Europe.

Council of Europe (2006) *Landscape Quality Objectives: From Theory to Practice.* Fifth meeting of the Workshops of the Council of Europe for the implementation of the European Landscape Convention, Strasbourg: Council of Europe.

Countryside Agency (2006) *Landscape: Beyond the View*. Cheltenham: Countryside Agency.

Creedy, J. B., Doran, H., Duffield, S. J., George, N. J., and Kass, G. S. (2009) *England's Natural Environment in 2060 – Issues, Implications and Scenarios*. Natural England Research Reports, Number 031. Sheffield: Natural England.

Cumming, G. S. (2011) 'Spatial resilience: integrating landscape ecology, resilience and sustainability', *Landscape Ecology*, 26: 899–909.

Cumulus (2009) *Area Schemes and Landscape Partnerships: Assembly of Output Data, Heritage Lottery Fund, 2008–9*. Broadway, Worcestershire: Cumulus Countryside and Rural Consultants.

Czerniak, J. (2007) 'Legibility and resilience', in J. Czerniak and G. Hargreaves (eds) *Large Parks*. New York: Princeton Architectural Press.

Davoudi, S., Crawford, J. and Mehmood, A. (eds) (2009) *Planning for Climate Change: Strategies for Mitigation and Adaptation for Spatial Planners*. London: Earthscan.

Dawson, D. (1994) *Are Habitat Corridors Conduits for Animals and Plants in a Fragmented Landscape? A review of the scientific evidence*. English Nature Research Report 94. Peterborough: English Nature.

de Groot, R. (2006) 'Function-analysis and valuation as a tool to assess land use conflicts in planning for sustainable, multi-functional landscapes', *Landscape and Urban Planning*, 75: 175–186.

de Groot, R. S., Wilson, M. and Boumans, R. (2002) 'A typology for the description, classification and valuation of ecosystem functions, goods and services', *Ecological Economics*, 41: 393–408.

Department for Environment, Food and Rural Affairs (Defra) (2010) *Adapting to Coastal Change: Developing a Policy Framework*. London: Defra.

Department for Transport (2008) *Building Sustainable Transport into New Developments: A Menu of Options for Growth Points and Eco-towns*. London: Defra.

Despommier, D. (2010) *The Vertical Farm: Feeding the World in the 21st Century*. New York: Thomas Dunne Books.

Dunnett, N. P. and Kingsbury, N. (2008) *Planting Green Roofs and Living Walls*, 2nd edition. Portland, OR: Timber Press.

Edelstein, M. R. (2004) *Contaminated Communities: Coping with Residential Toxic Exposure, 2nd Edition*. Boulder, CO: Westview Press/Perseus Books.

Edensor, T. (2000) 'Walking in the British countryside: reflexivity, embodied practices and ways to escape', *Body and Society*, 6: 81–106.

Edwards, C. (2009) *Resilient Nation: How Communities Respond to Systemic Breakdown*. London: Demos.

Eisenhauer, B. W., Krannich, R. S., and Blahna, D. J. (2000) 'Attachments to special places on public lands: an analysis of activities, reason for attachments, and community connections', *Society and Natural Resources*, 13: 421–441.

English Heritage (2000) *Power of Place: The Future of the Historic Environment*. London: English Heritage.

Environment Agency (2005) *Joining Up: Stockbridge Pathfinder*. Science report: SC010044/SR4. Bristol: Environment Agency.

Environment Agency (2008) *Sustainable Drainage Systems – An Introduction*. Bristol: Environment Agency.

Epstein, S. (1991) 'Cognitive-experiential self-theory: an integrative theory of personality', in R. C. Curtis (ed.) *The Relational Self: Theoretical Convergences in Psychoanalysis and Social Psychology*. New York: Guilford Press.

Erickson, D. L. (2004) 'Connecting corridors: implementing metropolitan greenway networks in North America', in R. H. G. Jongman and G. Pungetti (eds) *Ecological Networks and Greenways: Concepts, Design, Implementation*. Cambridge: Cambridge University Press.

European Environment Agency (EEA) (1995) *Europe's Environment: The Dobris Assessment*. Copenhagen: European Environment Agency.

Evans, E. P., Ashley, R., Hall, J. W., Penning-Rowsell, E. C., Saul, A., Sayers, P. B., Thorne, C. R. and Watkinson, A. R. (2004) *Foresight Future Flooding, Scientific Summary: Volume 1: Future Risks and Their Drivers*. London: Office of Science and Technology.

Fennell, D. (2008) *Ecotourism*, 3rd edition. Abingdon: Routledge.

Ford R. M. (2006), 'Social acceptability of forest management systems', unpublished PhD thesis, University of Melbourne.

Forest Research (2010) *Benefits of Green Infrastructure Case Study. Increasing species movement; Chattanooga Greenways, Tennessee, USA*. Farnham: Forest Research.

Foster, J., Lowe, A. and Winkelman, S. (2011) *The Value of Green Infrastructure for Urban Climate Adaptation*. Washington, DC: The Center for Clean Air Policy.

Fuller, R., Irvine, K. N., Devine-Wright, P., Warren, P. H. and Gaston, K. J. (2007) 'Psychological benefits of greenspace increase with biodiversity', *Biology Letters*, 3: 390–394.

Garmestani, A. S., Allen, C. R. and Gunderson, L. (2009) 'Panarchy: discontinuities reveal similarities in the dynamic system structure of ecological and social systems', *Ecology and Society* 14 (1): article 15. Available online at http://www.ecologyandsociety.org/vol14/iss1/art15/

Garnett, T. (2000) 'Urban agriculture in London: rethinking our food economy', in H. de Zeeuw, N. Bakker, M. Dubbeling, S. Gundel and U. Sabel-Koschella (eds) *Growing Cities, Growing Food*. Feldafing, German Foundation for International Development (DSE).

Gidlöf-Gunnarsson, A. and Öhrström, E. (2007) 'Noise and well-being in urban residential environments: the potential role of perceived availability to nearby green areas', *Landscape and Urban Planning*, 83: 115–126.

Gill, S., Handley, J. F., Ennos, A. R. and Pauleit, S. (2007) 'Adapting cities for climate change: the role of the green infrastructure', *Built Environment*, 33: 97–115.

Gill, S., Goodwin, C., Gowing, R., Lawrence, P., Pearson, J. and Smith, P. (2009) *Adapting to Climate Change: Creating Natural Resilience*. Technical report. London: Greater London Authority.

Gobster, P. H., Nassauer, J. I., Daniel, T. C. and Fry, G. (2007) 'The shared landscape: what does aesthetics have to do with ecology?' *Landscape Ecology*, 22: 959–972.

Graham, H., Mason, R. and Newman, A. (2009) *Literature Review: Historic Environment, Sense of Place, and Social Capital*. Commissioned for English Heritage. Newcastle: International Centre for Cultural and Heritage Studies (ICCHS), Newcastle University.

Grieve, Y., Sing, L., Ray, D. and Moseley, D. (2006) *Forest Habitat Networks Scotland, Broadleaved Woodland Specialist Network for SW Scotland*. Roslin, UK: Ecology Division Forest.

Grinde, B. (2009) 'Can the concept of discords help us find the causes of mental disease?', *Medical Hypothesis*, 73: 106–109.

Grinde, B. and Grindal Patil, G. (2009) 'Biophilia: does visual contact with nature impact on health and well-being?' *International Journal of Environmental Research and Public Health*, 6: 2332–2343.

Gunderson, L. and Holling, C.S. (eds) (2002) *Panarchy: Understanding Transformations in Human and Natural Systems*. Washington DC: Island Press.

Haines-Young, R. and Potschin, M. (2009) 'The links between biodiversity, ecosystem services and human well-being', in D. Raffaelli and C. Frid (eds) *Ecosystem Ecology: A New Synthesis*, Cambridge: Cambridge University Press, British Ecological Society Ecological Reviews Series.

Hartig, T., Böök, A., Garvill, J., Olsson, T. and Gärling, T. (1996) 'Environmental influences on psychological restoration', *Scandinavian Journal of Psychology*, 37: 378–393.

Haugan, L., Nyland, R., Fjeldavli, E., Meistad, T. and Braastad, B. O. (2006) 'Green care in Norway: farms as a resource for the educational, health and social sector', in J. Hassink and M. van Dijk (eds) *Farming for Health*, Dordrecht: Springer.

Hawkins, V. and Selman, P. (2002) 'Landscape scale planning: exploring alternative land use scenarios', *Landscape and Urban Planning*, 60: 211–224.

Hebbert, M. and Webb, B. (2011) 'Towards a liveable urban climate: lessons from Stuttgart', *ISOCARP Review*, 7: 120–137.

Henneberry, J., Rowley, S., Swanwick, C., Wells, F. and Burton, M. (2004) Creating a setting for investment. Report of a scoping study for South Yorkshire Forest Partnership and White Rose Forest. http://www.environment-investment.com/images/downloads/csi%20scoping%20study%20final%20report%20dec%2004.pdf (accessed 6 February 2012).

Herrington, S. (2006) 'Framed again: the picturesque aesthetics of contemporary landscapes', *Landscape Journal*, 25: 22–37.

Hilty, J. A., Lidicker Jr., W. Z. and Merenlender, A. M. (2006) *Corridor Ecology: The Science and Practice of Linking Landscapes for Biodiversity Conservation*, Washington: Island Press.

HM Government (2011) *The Natural Choice: Securing the Value of Nature* ('The Environment White Paper'). London: The Stationery Office.

Holling, C. S. and Gunderson, L. H. (2002) 'Resilience and adaptive cycles', in L. H. Gunderson and C. S. Holling (eds) *Panarchy: Understanding Transformations in Human and Natural Systems*. Washington DC: Island Press.

Hopkins, J. (2009) 'Adaptation of biodiversity to climate change: an ecological perspective', in M. Winter and M. Lobley (eds) *What is Land For? The food, fuel and climate change debate*, London: Earthscan.

Ingold, T. (1993) 'The temporality of the landscape', *World Archaeology*, 25: 152–174.

Jenkins, G., Murphy, J., Sexton, D., Lowe, J. Jones, P. and Kilsby, C. (2009) *Climate Projections: Briefing Report*, Exeter: Meteorological Office Hadley Centre.

Jenkins, K. M. and Boulton. A. J. (2003) 'Connectivity in a dryland river: short-term aquatic microinvertebrate recruitment following floodplain inundation', *Ecology*, 84: 2708–2723.

Jiggins, J., van Slobbe, E. and Röling, N. (2007) 'The organisation of social learning in response to perceptions of crisis in the water sector of The Netherlands', *Environmental Science and Policy*, 10: 526–536.

Jiven, G. and Larkham, P. J. (2003) 'Sense of place, authenticity and character: a commentary', *Journal of Urban Design*, 8: 67–81.

Johnson, J. and Rasker, R. (1995) 'The role of economic and quality of life values in rural business location', *Journal of Rural Studies*, 11: 405–416.

Jones, M. (2007) 'The European Landscape Convention and the question of public participation', *Landscape Research*, 32: 613–633.

Jongman, R. H. G. (2002) 'Homogenisation and fragmentation of the European landscape', *Landscape and Urban Planning*, 58: 211–221.

Jongman, R. H. G., Bouwma, I. M., Griffioen, A., Jones-Walters, L. and Van Doorn, A. M. (2011) 'The Pan European Ecological Network: PEEN', *Landscape Ecology*, 26: 311–326.

Jongman, R. H. G. and Pungetti, G. (eds) (2004) *Ecological Networks and Greenways: Concept, Design, Implementation*. Cambridge: Cambridge University Press.

Jorgensen, B. S. and Stedman, R. (2001) 'Sense of place as an attitude: lakeshore property owners' attitudes toward their properties', *Journal of Environmental Psychology*, 21: 233–248.

Jorgensen, B. S. and Stedman, R. C. (2006) 'A comparative analysis of predictors of sense of place dimensions: attachment to, dependence on, and identification with lakeshore properties', *Journal of Environmental Management*, 79: 316–327.

Kabat, P., van Vierssen, W., Veraart, J., Vellinga, P. and Aerts, J. (2006) 'Climate proofing The Netherlands', *Nature*, 438 (17): 285–286.

Kahn, P. H. Jr (1999) *The Human Relationship with Nature*. Cambridge, MA: MIT Press.

Kahn, P. H. Jr and Kellert, S. R. (eds) (2002) *Children and Nature: Psychological, Sociocultural, and Evolutionary Investigations*. Cambridge, MA: MIT Press.

Kaltenborn, B. P. and Williams D. R. (2002) 'The meaning of place: attachments to Femundsmarka National Park, Norway, among tourists and locals', *Norsk Geografisk Tidsskrift*, 56: 189–198.

Kaplan, S. (1992) 'The restorative environment: nature and human experience', in D. Relf (ed.) *The Role of Horticulture in Human Well-Being and Social Development: A National Symposium*, Portland, OR: Timber Press.

Kaplan, R. and Kaplan, S. (1989) *The Experience of Nature: A Psychological Perspective*. Cambridge: Cambridge University Press.

Keen, M., Brown, V. and Dyball, R. (eds) (2005) *Social Learning in Environmental Management: Towards a Sustainable Future*. London: Earthscan.

Kellert, S. R. (1993) 'The biological basis for human values of nature', in S. R. Kellert and E. O. Wilson (eds) *The Biophilia Hypothesis*, Washington, DC: Island Press.

Kent Wildlife Trust (on behalf of the Wildlife Trusts in the South East) (2006) *A Living Landscape for the South East: The Ecological Network Approach to Rebuilding Biodiversity for the 21st Century*. Maidstone: Kent Wildlife Trust.

Kienast, F., Bolliger, J., Potschin, M., de Groot, R. S., Verburg, P. H., Heller, I., Wascher, D. and Haines-Young, R. (2009) 'Assessing landscape functions with broad-scale environmental data: insights gained from a prototype development for Europe', *Environmental Management*, 44: 1099–1120.

Kondolf, G. M., Boulton, A. J., O'Daniel, S., Poole, G. C., Rahel, F. J., Stanley, E. H., Wohl, E., Bång, A., Carlstrom, J., Cristoni, C., Huber, H., Koljonen, S., Louhi, P. and Nakamura, K. (2006) 'Process-based ecological river restoration: visualizing three-dimensional connectivity and dynamic vectors to recover lost linkages', *Ecology and Society:* 11 (2): article 5. Available online at http://www.ecologyandsociety.org/vol11/iss2/art5/

Korpela, K. M. (1989) 'Place-identity as a product of environmental self-regulation', *Journal of Environmental Psychology*, 9: 241–256.

Korpela, K. M. (1991) 'Are favourite places restorative environments?', in J. Urbina-Soria, R. Ortega-Arideane and R. Bechtel (eds) *Healthy Environments*. Oklahoma City, OK: Environmental Design Research Association.

Korpela, K. and Hartig, T. (1996) 'Restorative qualities of favourite places', *Journal of Environmental Psychology*, 16: 221–233.

Korpela K. M., Hartig, T., Kaiser, G. F. and Fuhrer, U. (2001) 'Restorative experience and self-regulation in favorite places', *Environment and Behavior*, 33: 572–589.

Külvik, M. and Sepp, K. (2007) 'Ecological network experience from Estonia', in D. Hill (ed) *Making the Connections: A Role for Ecological Networks in Nature Conservation*, Proceedings of the 26th Conference of the Institute of Ecology and Environmental Management. Winchester, UK: Institute of Ecology and Environmental Management.

Kuo, F. E. and Sullivan, W. C. (2001) 'Environment and crime in the inner city: does vegetation reduce crime?', *Environment and Behavior*, 33: 343–365.

Lafortezza, R., Carrus, G., Sanesi, G. and Davies, C. (2009) 'Benefits and well-being perceived by people visiting green spaces in periods of heat stress', *Urban Forestry & Urban Greening*, 8: 97–108.

Land Use Consultants in association with Carol Trewin and Laura Mason (2006) *Exploration of the Relationship between Locality Foods and Landscape Character*. Report to the Countryside Agency, London: Land Use Consultants.

Landscape Character Network (2009) *European Landscape Convention 1: What does it Mean for Your Organisation?* Prepared for Natural England by Land Use Consultants. London: Land Use Consultants.

Landscape Institute (2009) *Green Infrastructure: Connected and Multifunctional Landscapes*. London: Landscape Institute.

Latimer, W. and Hill, D. (2008) 'Mitigation banking: securing no net loss for biodiversity?' *In Practice* (journal of the Institute of Ecology and Environmental Management), 62: 4–6.

Lawton, J. H., Brotherton, P. N. M., Brown, V. K., Elphick, C., Fitter, A. H., Forshaw, J., Haddow, R. W., Hilborne, S., Leafe, R. N., Mace, G. M., Southgate, M. P., Sutherland, W. A., Tew, T. E., Varley, J. and Wynne, G. R. (2010) *Making Space for Nature: A Review of England's Wildlife Sites and Ecological Network*. Report to the Department for Environment Food and Rural Affairs. London: Defra.

Le Dû-Blayo, L. (2011) 'How do we accommodate new land uses in traditional landscapes? Remanence of landscapes, resilience of areas, resistance of people', *Landscape Research*, 103: 417–434.

Lewicka, M. (2005) 'Ways to make people active: the role of place attachment, cultural capital, and neighbourhood ties', *Journal of Environmental Psychology*, 25: 381–395.

Livingston, M., Bailey, N. and Kearns, A. (2008) *People's Attachment to Place – The Influence of Neighbourhood Deprivation*. Report to the Joseph Rowntree Foundation. London: Chartered Institute of Housing.

London Climate Change Project (2009) *Adapting to Climate Change: Creating Natural Resilience*. London: Greater London Council.

Louv, R. (2005) *The Last Child in the Woods: Saving Our Children from Nature-deficit Disorder*. Chapel Hill, NC: Algonquin Books.

Lovell, S. T. (2010) 'Multifunctional urban agriculture for sustainable land use planning in the United States', *Sustainability*, 2: 2499–2522.

Lovell, S. T. and Johnston, D. M. (2009) 'Designing landscape for performance based on emerging principles in landscape ecology', *Ecology and Society*, 14 (1): article 44. Available online at http://www.ecologyandsociety.org/vol14/iss1/art44/

Maas, J., Spreeuwenberg, P., Van Winsum-Westra, M., Verheij, R. A., de Vries, S. and Groenewegen, P. (2009) 'Is green space in the living environment associated with people's feelings of social safety?', *Environment and Planning A*, 41: 1763–1777.

Mandler, J. M. (1984) *Stories, Scripts and Scenes: Aspects of Schema Theory*. Hillsdale, NJ: Laurence Earlbaum Associates.

Manzo, L. C. and Perkins, D. D. (2006) 'Finding common ground: the importance of place attachment to community participation and planning', *Journal of Planning Literature*, 20: 335–350.

Massey, D. B. (2005) *For Space*. London: Sage.

Matarrita-Cascante, D., Stedman, R. and Luloff, A. E. (2010) 'Permanent and seasonal residents' community attachment in natural amenity-rich areas: exploring the contribution of landscape-related factors', *Environment and Behavior*, 42: 197–220.

McFadden, L. (2010) 'Exploring systems interactions for building resilience within coastal environments and communities', *Environmental Hazards*, 9: 1–18.

Melby, P. and Cathcart, T. (2002) *Regenerative Design Techniques: Practical Applications in Landscape Design*. New York: Wiley.

Mels, T. (2005) 'Between "platial" imaginations and spatial rationalities: navigating justice and law in the low countries,' *Landscape Research*, 30: 321–335.

Mezirow, J. (1997) 'Transformative learning: theory to practice', *New Directions for Adult and Continuing Education*, 74: 5–12.

Milbrath, L. W. (1989) *Envisioning a Sustainable Society: Learning Our Way Out*. Albany NY: State University of New York Press.

Millennium Ecosystem Assessment (2005) *Ecosystems and Human Well-being: Synthesis*. Washington, DC: Island Press.

Miller, J. R. (2005) 'Biodiversity conservation and the extinction of experience', *TRENDS in Ecology and Evolution*, 20: 430–434.

Milligan, C. and Bingley, A. (2007) 'Therapeutic places or scary spaces? The impact of woodland on the mental well-being of young adults', *Health and Place*, 13: 799–811.

Mitchell, R. and Popham, F. (2009) 'Effect of exposure to natural environment on health inequalities: an observational population study', *Lancet*, 372: 1655–1660.

Morris, J. and Urry, J. (2006) *Growing Places: A Study of Social Change in The National Forest*. Farnham, UK: Forest Research.

Morris, N. (2003) *Health, Well-Being and Open Space: Literature Review*. Edinburgh: OPENspace (Edinburgh College of Art).

Mougeot, L. J. A. (2006) *Urban Agriculture for Sustainable Development*. Ottawa: International Development Research Centre.

Muro, M. and Jeffrey, P. (2008) 'A critical review of the theory and application of social learning in participatory natural resource management processes', *Journal of Environmental Planning and Management*, 51: 325–344.

Nanzer, B. (2004) 'Measuring sense of place: a scale for Michigan', *Administrative Theory and Praxis*, 26: 362–382.

Nassauer, J. I. (1997) 'Cultural sustainability: aligning aesthetics and ecology', in J. I. Nassauer (ed.) *Placing Nature: Culture and Landscape Ecology*, Washington, DC: Island Press.

Natural England (2009a) *Experiencing Landscapes: Capturing the 'Cultural Services' and 'Experiential Qualities' of Landscape*. Cheltenham: Natural England.

Natural England (2009b) *Green Growth for Green Communities*. A selection of regional case studies. ParkCity Conference 2009, Cheltenham: Natural England.

Natural England (2009c) *Green Infrastructure Guidance*. Cheltenham: Natural England.

Natural England (2009d) *Global Drivers of Change to 2060*. Commissioned report NECR030. Cheltenham: Natural England.

Natural England (2010) *Natural England's Position on 'All Landscapes Matter'*. Position statement. Cheltenham: Natural England.

Natural England (2011) *Natural England's Integrated Landscape Project (LIANE)*. Sheffield: Natural England.

Newton, J. (2007) *Wellbeing and the Natural Environment: A Brief Overview of the Evidence*. Bath: University of Bath.

Nicholls, S. and Crompton, J. L. (2005) 'The impact of greenways on property values: evidence from Austin, Texas', *Journal of Leisure Research*, 37: 321–341.

Nogue, J. (2006) 'The Spanish experience: landscape catalogues and landscape guidelines of Catalonia', in Council of Europe, *Landscape Quality Objectives: From Theory to Practice*. Fifth meeting of the Workshops of the Council of Europe for the implementation of the European Landscape Convention, Strasbourg: Council of Europe.

Norberg-Schulz, C. (1980) *Genius Loci, Towards a Phenomenology of Architecture*. New York: Rizzoli.

North West Climate Change Partnership (2011) *Green Infrastructure to Combat Climate Change: A Framework for Action in Cheshire, Cumbria, Greater Manchester, Lancashire, and Merseyside*. Prepared by Community Forests Northwest for the Northwest Climate Change Partnership, Warrington: Mersey Forest and others.

North West Green Infrastructure Think Tank (2009) *North West Green Infrastructure Guide*, version 1.1. Warrington: Mersey Forest and others.

North West Green Infrastructure Unit (2009) *Green Infrastructure Solutions to Pinch Point Issues in North West England: How Can Green Infrastructure Enable Sustainable Development?* Warrington: Mersey Forest and others.

O'Connell, P. E., Beven, K. J., Carney, J. N., Clements, R. O., Ewen, J., Fowler, H., Harris, G. L., Hollis, J., Morris, J., O'Donnell, G. M., Packman, J. C., Parkin, A., Quinn, P. F., Rose, S. C., Shepherd, M. and Tellier, S. (2004) *Review of Impacts of Rural Land Use And Management on Flood Generation – Impact Study Report*. Joint Defra/EA Flood and Coastal Erosion Risk Management R&D Programme, R&D Technical Report FD2114/TR. Defra: London.

Olwig, K. (1996) 'Recovering the substantive nature of landscape', *Annals of the Association of American Geographers*, 86: 630–653.

Olwig, K. (2008) 'Performing on the landscape versus doing landscape: perambulatory practice, sight and the sense of belonging', in T. Ingold and J. L. Vergunst (eds) *Ways of Walking: Ethnography and Practice on Foot*, Aldershot, UK: Ashgate Publishing.

Organisation for Economic Co-operation and Development (OECD) (eds) (1993) *OECD Core Set of Indicators for Environmental Performance Reviews.* Environment Monographs 83. Paris: OECD.

Parliamentary Office of Science and Technology (2011) *Landscapes of the Future.* POSTNOTE 380. London: POST.

Pauleit, S., Slinn, P., Handley, J. and Lindley, S. (2003) 'Promoting the natural greenstructure of towns and cities: English Nature's Accessible Natural Greenspace Standards Model', *Built Environment*, 29: 157–170.

Pellizzoni, L. (2001) 'The myth of the best argument: power, deliberation and reason', *British Journal of Sociology*, 52: 59–86.

Petts, J. (2001) *Urban Agriculture in London.* Copenhagen: World Health Organization Regional Office for Europe.

Petts, J. (2006) 'Managing public engagement to optimize learning: reflections from urban river restoration', *Human Ecology Review*, 13: 172–181.

Pigram, J. (1993) 'Human-nature relationships: leisure environments and natural settings', in T. Garling and R. Golledge (eds) *Behaviour and Environment: Psychological and Geographical Approaches*, Amsterdam: Elsevier Science Publishers.

Proshansky, H. M., Fabian, A. K. and Kaminoff, R. (1983) 'Place-identity: physical world socialization of the self', *Journal of Environmental Psychology*, 3: 57–83.

Putnam, R. D. (2000) *Bowling Alone: The Collapse and Revival of American Community.* New York: Simon and Schuster.

Pyle, R. M. (1978) 'The extinction of experience', *Horticulture*, 56: 64–67.

Ramos, I. L. (2010) 'Exploratory landscape scenarios in the formulation of landscape quality objectives', *Futures*, 42: 682–692.

Ravenscroft, N. and Taylor, B. (2009) 'Public engagement in the new productivism', in M. Winter and M. Lobley (eds) *What is Land For? The food, fuel and climate change debate.* London: Earthscan.

Ray, D. and Moseley, D. (2007) *A Forest Habitat Network for Edinburgh and the Lothians: The Contribution of Woodlands to Promote Sustainable Development Within the Regional Structure Plan.* Roslin, Midlothian: Forest Research.

Read, D. J., Freer-Smith, P. H., Morison, J. I. L., Hanley, N., West, C. C. and Snowdon, P. (eds) (2009) *Combating Climate Change – A Role for UK Forests. An assessment of the potential of the UK's trees and woodlands to mitigate and adapt to climate change.* Edinburgh: The Stationery Office.

Redman, C. L. and Kinzig, A. P. (2003) 'Resilience of past landscapes: resilience theory, society, and the *longue durée*', *Ecology and Society*, 7 (1): article 14. Available online at http://www.ecologyandsociety.org/vol7/iss1/art14/

Relph, E. (1976) *Place and Placelessness.* London: Pion.

Relph, E. (1981) *Rational Landscapes and Humanistic Geography.* London: Croom.

Roe, J. and Aspinall, P. (2011) 'The emotional affordances of forest settings: an investigation in boys with extreme behavioural problems', *Landscape Research*, 36: 535–552.

Rosenzweig, M. (2003) 'Reconciliation ecology and the future of species diversity', *Oryx*, 37: 194–205.

Rowley, S., Henneberry, J. and Stafford, T. (2008) Research Action 4.1 – Land Values, CSI research action 4.1 Final technical report. http://www.environment-investment.com/images/downloads/research_action_4.1_uk.pdf (accessed 6 February 2012).

Ryan, R. M. and Deci, E. L. (2000) 'Self-determination theory and the facilitation of intrinsic motivation, social development, and well-being', *American Psychologist*, 55: 68–78.

Scheffer, M., Carpenter, S., Foley, J. A., Folke, C. and Walker, B. (2001) 'Catastrophic shifts in ecosystems', *Nature*, 413: 591–596.

Schneeberger, N., Bürgi, M., Hersperger, A. and Ewald, K. (2007) 'Driving forces and rates of landscape change as a promising combination for landscape change research – an application on the northern fringe of the Swiss Alps', *Land Use Policy*, 24: 349–361.

Schusler, T. M., Decker, D. J. and Pfeffer, M. J. (2003) 'Social learning for collaborative natural resource management', *Society and Natural Resources*, 15: 309–326.

Scott, A., Christie, M. and Tench, H. (2003) 'Visitor payback: panacea or Pandora's box for conservation in the UK?', *Journal of Environmental Planning and Management*, 46: 583–604.

Selman, P. (2006) *Planning at the Landscape Scale*. London: Routledge.

Selman, P. (2007) 'Sustainability at the national and regional scales', in J. Benson and M. Roe (eds) *Landscape and Sustainability*, 2nd edition. London: Routledge.

Selman, P. (2008) 'What do we mean by sustainable landscape?', *Sustainability: Science, Practice, & Policy*, 4 (2). Available online at http://sspp.proquest.com/archives/vol4iss2/communityessay.selman.html

Selman, P. (2009) 'Planning for landscape multifunctionality', *Sustainability: Science, Practice, & Policy*, 5 (2). Available online at http://sspp.proquest.com/archives/vol5iss2/communityessay.pselman.html

Selman, P. (2010a) 'Learning to love the landscapes of carbon-neutrality', *Landscape Research*, 35: 157–171.

Selman, P. (2010b) 'Landscape planning – preservation, conservation and sustainable development', *Town Planning Review*, 81: 382–406.

Selman, P. (2012) 'Landscapes as integrating frameworks for human, environmental and policy processes', in T. Plieninger and C. Bieling (eds) *Resilience and the Cultural Landscape: Understanding and Managing Change in Human-Shaped Environments*, Cambridge: Cambridge University Press.

Selman, P. and Knight, M. (2006) 'On the nature of virtuous change in cultural landscapes: exploring sustainability through qualitative models', *Landscape Research*, 31: 295–308.

Selman, P., Carter, C., Lawrence, A. and Morgan, C. (2010) 'Re-connecting with a neglected river through imaginative engagement', *Ecology and Society*, 15 (3): article 18. Available online at http://www.ecologyandsociety.org/vol15/iss3/art18/

Shamai, S. and Kellerman, A. (1985) 'Conceptual and experimental aspects of regional awareness: an Israeli case study', *Tijdschrift voor Economische en Sociale Geografie*, 76: 88–99.

Shamai, S. and Ilatov, Z. (2005) 'Measuring sense of place: methodological aspects', *Tijdschrift voor Economicshe en Sociale Geographie*, 96: 467–476.

Smith J. W., Davenport, M. A., Anderson, D. H. and Leahy, J. E. (2011) 'Place meanings and desired management outcomes', *Landscape and Urban Planning*, 101: 359–370.

Smith, M., Moseley, D., Chetcuti, J. and de Ioanni, M. (2008) Glasgow and Clyde Valley Integrated Habitat Networks. Report to Glasgow and Clyde Valley Green Network Partnership. Edinburgh: Forestry Commission.

Stedman, R. C. (2002) 'Towards a social psychology of place: predicting behavior from place-based cognitions, attitude, and identity', *Environment and Behavior*, 34: 561–581.

Stedman, R. C. (2003) 'Is it *really* just a social construction: the contribution of the physical environment to sense of place', *Society and Natural Resources*, 16: 671–685.

Stephenson, J. (2007) 'The cultural values model: an integrated approach to values in landscapes', *Landscape and Urban Planning*, 84: 127–139.

Taylor, J. J., Brown, D. G. and Larsen, L. (2007) 'Preserving natural features: a GIS-based evaluation of a local open-space ordinance', *Landscape and Urban Planning*, 82: 1–16.

Termorshuizen, J. W. and Opdam, P. (2009) 'Landscape services as a bridge between landscape ecology and sustainable development', *Landscape Ecology*, 24: 1037–1052.

Thomas, C. D., Cameron, A., Green, R. E., Bakkenes, M., Beaumont, L. J., Collingham, Y. C., Erasmus, B. F. N., Ferreira de Siqueira, M., Grainger, A., Hannah, L., Hughes, L., Huntley, B., van Jaarsveld, A. S., Midgley, G. F., Miles, L., Ortega-Huerta, M. A., Peterson, A. T., Phillips, O. L. and Williams, S.E. (2004) 'Extinction risk from climate change', *Nature*, 427: 145–148.

Tippett, J. (2004) 'Think like an ecosystem – embedding a living system paradigm into participatory planning', *Systemic Practice and Action Research*, 17: 603–622.

Town and Country Planning Association (2004) *Biodiversity by Design: A Guide for Sustainable Communities*. London: TCPA.

Trumper, K., Bertzky, M., Dickson, B., van der Heijden, G., Jenkins, M. and Manning, P. (2009) *The Natural Fix? The role of ecosystems in climate mitigation. A UNEP rapid response assessment*. Cambridge, UK: United Nations Environment Programme, UNEPWCMC.

Trust for Public Land (2008) *How Much Value Does the City of Philadelphia Receive from its Park and Recreation System?* A report by the Trust for Public Land's Center for City Park Excellence, San Francisco, CA: Trust for Public Land.

Tuan, Y.-F. (1977) *Space and Place: The Perspective of Experience*. Minneapolis, MN: University of Minnesota Press.

Turner, T. (1995) 'Greenways, blueways, skyways and other ways to a better London', *Landscape and Urban Planning*, 33: 269–282.

Turner, T. (2006) 'Greenway planning in Britain: recent work and future plans', *Landscape and Urban Planning*, 76: 240–251.

Twigger-Ross, C. L. and Uzzell D. I. (1996) 'Place and identity processes', *Journal of Environmental Psychology*, 16: 205–220.

Tzoulas,K., Korpela, K., Venn, S., Yli-Pelkonen, V., Kaźmierczak, A., Niemela, J. and James, P. (2007) 'Promoting ecosystem and human health in urban areas using green infrastructure: a literature review', *Landscape and Urban Planning*, 81: 167–178.

Ulrich, R. S. (1981) 'Natural versus urban scenes: some psychophysiological effects', *Environment and Behavior*, 13: 523–556.

Ulrich, R. S. (1983) 'Aesthetic and affective response to natural environment', in I. Altman and J. F. Wohlwill (eds) *Human Behaviour and Environment: Advances in Theory and Research. Volume 6: Behaviour and the Natural Environment*. New York: Plenum Press.

Ulrich, R. S. (1984) 'View through window may influence recovery from surgery', *Science*, 224: 420–421.

Ulrich, R. S. (1992) 'Influences of passive experiences with plants on individual wellbeing and health', in D. Relf (ed) *The Role of Horticulture in Human Well-Being and Social Development: A National Symposium*. Portland, OR: Timber Press.

Ulrich, R. S. (1999) 'Effects of gardens on health outcomes: theory and research', in C. Cooper-Marcus and M. Barnes (eds) *Healing Gardens: Therapeutic Benefits and Design Recommendations*. New York: John Wiley.

Valett, H. M., Fisher, S. G., Grimm, N. B. and Camill, P. (1994) 'Vertical hydrologic exchange and ecological stability of a desert stream ecosystem', *Ecology*, 75: 548–560.

van den Born, R. J. G., Lenders, R. H. J., De Groot, W. T. and Huijsman, E. (2001) 'The new biophilia: an exploration of visions of nature in Western countries', *Environmental Conservation*, 28: 65–75.

Velarde, M. D., Fry, G. and Tveit, M. (2007) 'Health effects of viewing landscapes – landscape types in environmental psychology', *Urban Forestry and Urban Greening*, 6: 199–212.

Viljoen, A., Bohn, K. and Howe, J. (eds) (2005) *Continuous Productive Urban Landscapes. Designing urban agriculture for sustainable cities*. London: Architectural Press.

Vuorinen, R. (1990) 'Persoonallisuus ja minuus [Personality and self]', *Journal of Environmental Psychology*, 11, 201–230.

Waldheim, C. (2006) (ed.) *The Landscape Urbanism Reader*. New York: Princeton Architectural Press.

Walker, B. and Salt, D. (2006) *Resilience Thinking: Sustaining Ecosystems and People in a Changing World*. Washington, DC: Island Press.

Walker, B., Carpenter, S., Anderies, J., Abel, N., Cumming, G., Janssen, M., Lebel, L., Norberg, J., Peterson, G. D. and Pritchard, R. (2002) 'Resilience management in social–ecological systems: a working hypothesis for a participatory approach', *Ecology and Society*, 6 (1): article 14. Available online at http://www.ecologyandsociety.org/vol6/iss1/art14/.

Walker, B., Holling, C. S., Carpenter, S. R. and Kinzig, A. (2004) 'Resilience, adaptability and transformability in social–ecological systems', *Ecology and Society*, 9 (2): article 5. Available online at http://www.ecologyandsociety.org/vol9/iss2/

Ward Thompson, C. (2011) 'Linking landscape and health: the recurring theme', *Landscape and Urban Planning*, 99: 187–195.

Warnock, S. and Brown, N. (1998) 'A vision for the countryside', *Landscape Design*, 269: 22–26.

Watts, K., Humphrey, J., Griffiths, M., Quine, C., and Ray, D. (2005) *Evaluating Biodiversity in Fragmented Landscapes: Principles*, Information Note 73. Edinburgh: Forestry Commission.

Weick, K. E. (1995) *Sensemaking in Organisations*. Thousand Oaks, CA: Sage Publications Inc.

Wheater, H. and Evans, E. (2009) 'Land use, water management and future flood risk', *Land Use Policy*, 26S: S251–S264.

The Wildlife Trusts (2007) *A Living Landscape for the South East. The ecological network approach to rebuilding biodiversity for the 21st century*. Maidstone: Kent Wildlife Trust.

The Wildlife Trusts (2009) *A Living Landscape: A Call to Restore the UK's Battered Ecosystems, for Wildlife and People*. Newark, UK: The Wildlife Trusts.

Willemen, L., Hein, L., van Mensvoort, M. E. F. and Verburg, P. H. (2010) 'Space for people, plants, and livestock? Quantifying interactions among multiple landscape functions in a Dutch rural region', *Ecological Indicators*, 19: 62–73.

Williams, K., Joynt, J. L. R. and Hopkins, D. (2010) 'Adapting to climate change in the compact city: the suburban challenge', *Built Environment*, 36: 105–115.

Wilson, E. O. (1984) *Biophilia*. Cambridge, MA: Harvard University Press.

Winn, J., Tierney, M., Heathwaite, L., Jones, L., Paterson, J., Simpson, L., Thompson, A. and Turley, C. (2011) 'The drivers of change in UK ecosystems and ecosystem services', in *The UK National Ecosystem Assessment Technical Report*. UK National Ecosystem Assessment, Cambridge, UK: UNEP-WCMC.

Wohl, E. (2004) *Disconnected Rivers: Linking Rivers to Landscapes*. New Haven, CT: Yale University Press.

Wood, J. D., Richardson, R. I., Scollan, N. D., Hopkins, A., Dunn, R., Buller, H. and Whittington, F. M. (2007) 'Quality of meat from biodiverse grassland', in J. J. Hopkins, A. J. Duncan, D. I. McCracken, S. Peel and J. R. B. Tallowin (eds) *High Value Grassland*. Cirencester, UK: British Grassland Society.

Woodroffe, C. D. (2007) 'The natural resilience of coastal systems: primary concepts', in L. McFadden, E. Penning-Rowsell and R. J. Nicholls (eds) *Managing Coastal Vulnerability*. Amsterdam: Elsevier.

Wylie, J. W. (2007) *Landscape*. Abingdon, UK: Routledge.

Index

Figures, tables and boxes are indicated with an italic 'f', 't', or 'b' after the locator. For example: biophilia 7-13, 89f.
Main coverage of a topic is indicated with a bolded locator, for example: change drivers 42-7.